M000012669

"*Secrets of a Mid-Life Mom* should be required reading for every mother who is raising children when her peers are planning for an empty nest, a fulfilling career advancement, or an early retirement. Well researched, fun to read, and practical to the core, Jane Jarrell reveals her best advice for thriving as a mid-life mom."

— CAROL KENT
president, Speak Up Speaker Services;
international speaker and author

"Those of us living this new trend of delayed motherhood need all the encouragment we can get. Jane's insight and sagelike advice rings with authenticity. *Secrets of a Mid-life Mom* hits the target!"

— LINDSEY O'CONNOR
mid-life mom of five from crib to college;
author of *If Mama Goes South, We're All Going With Her*

"Every woman wants a friend who can respond to her concerns with, 'I know how you feel.' Jane Jarrell is that friend for mid-life moms."

— BRENDA POINSETT
director of retreats for mid-life women;
author of *What Will I Do for the Rest of My Life?*

"What an endearing mix of cheeky wit and gut level honesty! It's full of clever insights and poignant confessions regarding the challenges of mothering beyond our twenties. Just the shot of encouragement that mothers everywhere need!"

— JULIE BARNHILL
best-selling author of *She's Gonna Blow* and *Scandalous Grace*

"In her not-for-sissies approach, Jane offers a refreshing truth, frankness, and grace for every woman who's up for the noble challenge of motherhood. And why not? Mothers are, hands down, the most influential people on the planet."

—VIRELLE KIDDER
conference speaker; author of *Donkeys Still Talk*

"Jane Jarrell speaks to moms from her own mid-life mom journey with practical wisdom for the way."

—ELISA MORGAN
president, MOPS International

"If anyone needs secrets for living it's the mid-life mom. Jane does a great job of identifying the struggle, but not leaving us in the middle of it. She gives us a way through it. If you want to come out strong on the other side, you need to read *Secrets of a Mid-Life Mom*."

—ANITA LUSTREA
host and producer of *Midday Connection*, Moody Broadcasting

Secrets *of a*

Mid-Life

Mom

JANE JARRELL

NAVPRESS®

BRINGING TRUTH TO LIFE

OUR GUARANTEE TO YOU

We believe so strongly in the message of our books that we are making this quality guarantee to you. If for any reason you are disappointed with the content of this book, return the title page to us with your name and address and we will refund to you the list price of the book. To help us serve you better, please briefly describe why you were disappointed. Mail your refund request to: NavPress, P.O. Box 35002, Colorado Springs, CO 80935.

The Navigators is an international Christian organization. Our mission is to reach, disciple, and equip people to know Christ and to make Him known through successive generations. We envision multitudes of diverse people in the United States and every other nation who have a passionate love for Christ, live a lifestyle of sharing Christ's love, and multiply spiritual laborers among those without Christ.

NavPress is the publishing ministry of The Navigators. NavPress publications help believers learn biblical truth and apply what they learn to their lives and ministries. Our mission is to stimulate spiritual formation among our readers.

© 2004 by Jane Jarrell

All rights reserved. No part of this publication may be reproduced in any form without written permission from NavPress, P.O. Box 35001, Colorado Springs, CO 80935.
www.navpress.com

NAVPRESS, BRINGING TRUTH TO LIFE, and the NAVPRESS logo are registered trademarks of NavPress. Absence of ® in connection with marks of NavPress or other parties does not indicate an absence of registration of those marks.

ISBN 1-57683-458-1

Cover design by Brand Navigation, LLC (The Office of Bill Chiaravalle) www.brandnavigation.com
Cover photo by PhotoDisc/Steve Gardner, His Image Pixelworks
Creative Team: Terry Behimer, Anita Palmer, Rachelle Gardner, Darla Hightower, Glynese Northam

Some names have been changed; otherwise all of the anecdotes and personal stories in this book are true.

Unless otherwise identified, all Scripture quotations in this publication are taken from the HOLY BIBLE: NEW INTERNATIONAL VERSION® (NIV®). Copyright © 1973, 1978, 1984 by International Bible Society. Used by permission of Zondervan Publishing House. All rights reserved. Other versions used include: THE MESSAGE (MSG). Copyright © 1993, 1994, 1995, 1996, 2000, 2001, 2002. Used by permission of NavPress Publishing Group; the New American Standard Bible (NASB), © The Lockman Foundation 1960, 1962, 1963, 1968, 1971, 1972, 1973, 1975, 1977; the Contemporary English Version (CEV) © 1995 by American Bible Society. Used by permission.; and the King James Version (KJV).

Jarrell, Jane Cabaniss, 1961-
  Secrets of a mid-life mom / Jane Jarrell.
    p. cm.
Includes bibliographical references.
  ISBN 1-57683-458-1
  1. Middle aged mothers. 2. Motherhood--Religious
aspects--Christianity. I. Title.
  HQ759.43.J37 2004
  306.874'3'0844--dc22
                              2003023816

Printed in Canada

2 3 4 5 6 7 8 9 10 11 / 09 08 07 06 05

FOR A FREE CATALOG OF
NAVPRESS BOOKS & BIBLE STUDIES,
CALL 1-800-366-7788 (USA)
OR 1-800-839-4769 (CANADA)

Dedication

For my husband

One of the biggest secrets of a mid-life mom is having a supportive mid-life dad.

This is for you, Mark. First, without you I would not be a mom and second, without your love I would have no secrets to share.

Contents

Foreword

By Ellie Kay

Call me eccentric, but there were two things I wanted to do in life before I hit forty: 1. have twins and 2. go skydiving. Okay, don't call me eccentric, call me crazy! Well, I'm a mom of seven children, including five school-aged children and two young adult children — and there's nary a twin among them. As the big 4–O loomed in the future, my husband made it clear that mirror-image babies were not going to be a part of our family photo album. So, I did what any other "almost-forty-mom-who-wants-to-make-her-dream-come-true" would do. I jumped out of an airplane at 10,000 feet.

In retrospect, my husband Bob said if given a choice, he would have picked twins. Even though he's a fighter pilot in the U.S. Air Force, he had no idea how nerve wracking it would be for him when he realized I was going tandem skydiving. He simply could not relate to jumping out of a perfectly good airplane. I went on my big adventure after a bookseller's convention, and Bob waited anxiously by the phone to hear that I had landed in one piece. When I finally made the fateful call, Bob was shouting, "Do you have any idea what I went through? Do you know what it's like to plan a memorial service in your mind?" I let him calm down and the next day I reminded him,

"What you went through yesterday is exactly how I feel every time you strap on that fighter jet for Uncle Sam!"

Life as a mid-life mom is something like jumping out of an airplane or being married to a man who flies them in hostile territory and into the great unknown. But if you are confident in the security of your parachute and you know who has your back, it can be a beautiful adventure. It is so quiet at 10,000 feet and you can seemingly see the entire world as you drift slowly back to earth.

Take it from me, skydiving and mothering in your mid-years are not activities for the weak at heart or faint of spirit. Jane Jarrell helps young-at-heart but older-in-years moms learn to celebrate their unique challenges with a sense of adventure.

Jane offers the candid perspective of an experienced jumper who has taken a flying leap of faith and landed in one piece. I particularly love the way "Can-Do Jane" admits that she's sometimes a "No-Way Jane." It's validating to know that even someone with as much on the ball as Jane can have the typically challenging days that all moms have. Maybe it's because she knows firsthand what it's like to have the cat eat the goldfish, and a toddler who just gets the hang of potty training on the same day the toilet goes on the blink.

I truly enjoyed this book and believe that you will, too. It's a celebration of mothering for moms thirty-something and beyond. Grab your children by the hand (or plop them down in front of VeggieTales) and take a flying faith-filled leap into the great unknown of parenting in mid-life.

Ellie Kay, best-selling author of *Heroes at Home,*

The New Bride Guide, and *A Woman's Guide to Family Finances*

Acknowledgments

My heartfelt thanks goes to Mark and Sarah for hanging in there with me when the deadlines were looming. Without the two of you, there would be no book. Thank you for loving me.

Thank you, Mom and Dad, for your prayers, support, and help during my whole life.

To R. J. and Edwina and our prayer group, thank you for your encouragement and prayers.

AWSA ladies, Advanced Writers and Speakers Association, your love and kindness allowed me to navigate some rough waters during this project. You are a testimony to the quote "Christians are like snowflakes: Alone, they are just one of a kind figures; but when they stick together they can stop traffic." Thanks for sticking with me. Thank you, Linda Evans Shepard, for making this fellowship a reality.

Terry Behimer, thank you for taking a chance with me. Your professionalism and positive approach have been a breath of fresh air to this mid-life mom.

Rachelle Gardner, thank you for stepping in and taking the baton to the finish line. Another professional with a heart for God. Thank you for taking the manuscript and making a real book out of it. You were encouraging, on target, and kind.

The staff at NavPress, thank you for the love and support you showed during the personal "bumps in the road" as I worked on this project.

Last but definitely not least—the brunch bunch, Kelly, Holly, Susan, Kim, and Robyn. Thank you for your time, valuable input, and friendship. If I ever write Secrets of an Old Mom, I want you all to come to another brunch of soft foods with lots of fiber.

Introduction

So here you are at mid-life — and if you're reading this you likely have a child or two running around. Right now, someone under three feet tall is probably tugging on your sleeve whining, "Mommmmmmmy!" And you're despairing that you won't even have a chance to read one paragraph in peace. At this very moment, your car is strewn with cheesy goldfish, you owe ten people thank-you notes, the playroom has been declared a federal disaster site, and you just want to take a nap. Sister, I know where you are. I'm only able to write this because the rest of my family is blissfully asleep. And no — I didn't drug them! (Although the thought has crossed my mind as writing deadlines approached.) It's early in the morning, dawn is breaking over the horizon, and I'm in the middle of my first cup of French Roast. It's that time of day when I'm grateful for all my blessings, and I thank God for making me a mid-life mom.

Reality check — these serene moments are the exception. The last several years have been a struggle: from becoming a mommy in the first place, to redefining myself as the symbiotic other-half of a little one, while still being the other-half of my husband (how many halves do I have?), and trying to figure out how to maintain the career I've spent the better part of two decades building. Then there's the age and mortality thing. Turning forty hit me like a ton of Legos, although I know it's not the same for everyone. Some women get hit at thirty-nine, others not until forty-nine. (Are there any women who never get hit? I'd like to meet them!) But statistically, my life is half over and here I am with a young child, wondering if I know what in the world I'm doing.

Mid-life moms. Who are we? And do we really need to talk about this? I like to say we're savvy women over thirty-five who have traveled different roads that delayed our childrearing. Many of us have made difficult choices and accomplished remarkable things. We're healthier women than ever before; we are more educated; we are experienced, many of us with established careers. Some of us are in the trenches of motherhood while helping our parents face the challenges of aging. When you think about it, mid-life moms are pretty amazing. We're the supreme multitaskers, all-too-familiar with words like balance, juggling, and time management. We all share the challenges of keeping one eye on little ones and the other on our retirement plans.

Although I have a whole circle of friends made up of mid-life moms, I also spend time with moms half my age. I can't help but notice the wide age range of moms with young kids. A generation ago (that is, when I was growing up) moms seemed to have so much in common. They were all in their twenties, they married early, had children soon after, and in most cases, didn't have careers during that time. Today it's all over the map. First-time moms range in age from early twenties to early forties and have widely divergent backgrounds and family situations. I've found it necessary (for my mental health) to seek out other moms on the high end of that age spectrum because, although all moms share the common experience of parenting, the journey feels so much different now than it would have fifteen years ago.

Most of us on the topside of forty find ourselves increasingly thinking about the bigger issues such as The Meaning of Life. We're gaining wisdom, maturing spiritually, and we're concerned with making our lives count. All this while passing graham crackers to the back seat of the car—motherhood isn't what it used to be!

We live in a social climate that makes it more common than ever before to have children later in life. Couples are exercising "wait control," with first-time mothers over thirty-five a rapidly growing demographic.[1] While most first-time moms are still between the ages of twenty and thirty-four, the average age of a woman giving birth for the first time has been steadily increasing over the last thirty-five years. Delaying parenthood is the new norm, even among Christians. In 2001, nearly 100,000 first-time mothers gave birth between the ages of forty and forty-four.[2] America's moms have indeed become the nation's "ladies in waiting."[3]

There seem to be several interlocking causes and influencers of this trend. Women are delaying motherhood to pursue education and careers. First-time birthrates for women in their late thirties to forties with a college degree were much higher than the rates for women with less education.[4] In 2002, *USA Today* reported that labor-force participation among new mothers dropped for the first time in nearly twenty-five years. A more secure financial situation and a better education make taking time off from work a more viable option.

New medical technologies have extended the childbearing years. Couples who delay parenthood are more likely to experience infertility, but the medical options keep expanding our choices, and most of us find a way to become parents one way or another. We're living longer than in the past, too. All this adds up to a noticeable trend.

"Our expectations have stretched," says Nancy Marshall, a senior scientist at the Center for Research on Women at Wellesley College in Massachusetts. "The baby boomers are aging, so society is upping its definition of what's an older parent. Over 30 used to be considered an elderly first-time pregnancy. This got moved to 35, now it's more like 40."[5]

Obviously, the media and entertainment industries are a pervasive influence. (Does Hollywood reflect life or does life reflect Hollywood?) Increasingly, mid-life motherhood is becoming glamorized by celebrity mothers—certainly not the role models most of us aspire to, but nevertheless, conspicuous proof that it can be done. Twenty-five years ago Yoko Ono made big news when she became a mother over forty. Now Madonna, Jamie Lee Curtis, Celine Dion, Rosie O'Donnell, Jodi Foster, and many others have started motherhood later in life, often without bothering to bring along a mid-life dad. With their nannies, housekeepers, and personal assistants, they make it all appear so easy.

But for us mere mortals, perception and expectations can hit motherhood smack in the face. Having had nearly four decades in the "me" generation, we can feel pretty out-of-control when we suddenly enter the world where "me" is entwined with what "someone else" needs. Accustomed to being in charge of our own destinies, we find it difficult to make unpleasant choices, like giving up our hard-won career versus going back to work and leaving our child with a caregiver. For Christians, expectations seem even higher. Traditional women's groups and Bible studies can leave us with a feeling that if we don't fit into a rigid (and often inaccurate) interpretation of the Proverbs 31 woman as The Perfect Homemaker, we're somehow failing our husbands, our children, and God.

For some mid-life mothers, going from the boardroom to Barney puts us way outside our comfort zone. For others, experiencing early signs of menopause while shuttling kids to preschool causes us to wake up and smell the coffee—we're not getting any younger. The mid-life mom also can be a "mom in the middle," sandwiched between meeting the needs of her young children and taking care of her aging parents.

Because mid-life parenting is a new trend, we don't have any previous generations to rely on for help and advice on the unique aspects of our parenting journey. Our mothers can't help us learn how to balance a hard-earned career with a hard-earned baby. Past generations don't have much experience with handling hot flashes while changing diapers. Our grandmas didn't have gray hair until they were actually grandmas. So we're not few in numbers, but we're pioneering women, forging new territory on the mommy expedition. And that's why I think we like to talk about it.

In the process of researching this book, people have asked why I think so many women are choosing to become moms later in life. The answer, I think, lies in the misunderstood notion of "choice." Did I really choose to wait until I was thirty-five to have my first child? No—it seems God had a plan for my life. He chose my husband and the timing of my marriage, He blessed me with a career, He allowed me to grapple with infertility and miscarriage, and finally, He gifted me with parenthood. He knew what was best for me and arranged the circumstances of my life accordingly. So while the statistics and the media may be able to identify all the reasons for the mid-life mothering trend, most of us who are stuck in the middle of it realize it was never a conscious choice—it was simply the way things turned out. We ultimately come to a place of trust in the Lord's goodness and sovereignty, and rest in gratitude for the way He's arranged our lives.

In the following chapters, we'll look at secrets many mid-life mothers have revealed that make their complicated lives work more successfully. We'll talk about the things we share with mothers of all ages and the things that set us apart. My goal is to shed light on the unique and wonderful (and sometimes terrifying) experience we're going through, while offering support, solid advice, and a few laughs along the way.

The transition from youth to over-forty has been tough for me at times. This book grew out of my own struggles as well as conversations with other women, all mid-life moms but each with her own unique journey. It is my prayer that you will find encouragement in these pages and that your appreciation for the gift of being a mid-life mom will increase, as mine has. With the apostle Paul, "I pray also that the eyes of your heart may be enlightened in order that you may know the hope to which he has called you,"[6] that wonderful hope in Christ that gets us through each day.

I feel as though I am sitting down with you over a grande latte at Starbucks and visiting about mid-life concerns—from wrinkle creams to long-held dreams. So, grab that cup of coffee and let's get started.

1

Brunch Bunch

THE TOP TEN SECRETS OF MID-LIFE MOMS

Sally, forty-six and a mother of four, wrestles with the joys and challenges every mid-life mother faces, but she realizes she is at her best when she has support from friends.

> *I just realized the other day I was at mid-life. My youngest is two. Chasing after him is just a small part of my very full day. Some days are harried, what with four kids, a business I work from home, shopping, housework, cooking, nurturing, and church responsibilities. Some days I want to stop the merry-go-round and run to the nearest beach with a good book and a big diet drink. But this is my life, so I want to live it well.*
>
> *My secret is surrounding myself with positive people who have that "can-do" attitude. Sure I get tired (let's face it—I'm exhausted). But the community I feel with other mothers helps me through my trials and troubles. We share, don't compare, and bask in the journey together.*
>
> *We also remind each other what's important: Surround yourself with friends, live your priorities, choose to live life with*

everything you've got. Watch and wait for God's next miracle in you. Our attitude is a choice we make every day.

Sally chooses to manage her complicated life with a positive attitude and a band of fellow sojourners who can share with her the secrets of their success. I try to do the same—and as I was writing this book, it quickly became obvious that my best resource was my friends. I could send out an e-mail asking mid-life-mom questions, and boom!—my mailbox was filled with honesty, wisdom, and truth I couldn't have paid for. When I was wrestling with a challenge, I could call up a mid-life mom buddy and we'd talk it out. In the mornings I walk with my LOT group—the Ladies on Track, as we call ourselves because we walk a track—and the time together always provides me with inspiration, food for thought, and a few laughs thrown in. Hanging out with this group really gave me the motivation and the raw material to write about mid-life moms.

I recently decided to host a brunch for some mid-life mothers who have made a huge difference in my life and who have been sharing their "secrets" with me all along. We talked about everything from fried nerves to fried chicken, from not being too chicken to say no, to bravely saying yes to our stage in life. Besides the celebration of our friendship, the purpose of this brunch was to boil down the essence of the whole mid-life mom thing. What were the best parts? Are there any downsides?

My "brunch bunch" laughed about articles and media reports describing the new trend of "older" mothers. From what they say, you'd think we spend all our time worrying about being old and sick by the time our kids are in college. Or that we're suffering through hellacious mid-life crises while pretending to be soccer moms. But at least as far as my friends are concerned, that's just not the case. All the moms I've talked to have definite strategies for making their lives work as well as possible. Do we always get it right? Not by a long shot! But for the most part, we realize we need to rely on God, each other, and the special strengths of "mid-life" to get us through. The brunch bunch boiled it down to The Top Ten Secrets of Mid-life Moms—and here they are.

Mid-Life Mom *Secret 10*

"Our friends keep us sane."

I've already mentioned the importance of friends, but I'm going to say right now that I think they're one of the best secrets of mid-life moms. They might not all be mid-life moms like you. You may not have a large circle—one or two good buddies will do. But we're more susceptible to depression, stress, and burnout when we haven't spent enough time nurturing friendships. Husbands and children may be higher on the priority list, but what husband is going to tell you honestly when that dress really *does* make you look fat? Face it, when you're getting whiny about the trials of your life, your friends will sympathize just the right amount before telling you to snap out of it—and you're just not going to take that from darling hubby! As Ecclesiastes 4:10 (CEV) says, "If you fall, your friend can help you up. But if you fall without having a friend nearby, you are really in trouble."

Mid-life mom Kris has been learning the hard way the surprising importance of having friends with whom you share some life characteristics. At forty-two, she just gave birth to her fourth child. This in itself sets her apart from most of her similar-age friends, who have one or two children each, but the fact that she homeschools adds to the differences. This pregnancy has been fraught with emotional difficulties, as she has tackled the daily challenges of a large family and the homeschooling lifestyle, without the support of friends in a similar situation. Many times she has felt lost and alone, not because she doesn't have friends who love her, but because her particular circle of friends can't offer her the special kind of support that comes from having "been there." While Kris loves her pals, she is beginning to realize that she's going to have to actively pursue some new relationships in order to get the support she needs. She's looking into local mom's clubs, church groups, and homeschooling organizations, where she might find more moms who share similar daily circumstances. I think her story illustrates that God gives us friends not just to make life more fun, but because without them life can become excruciatingly difficult.

My brunch bunch agreed that our friendships are definitely one of the most important elements in making our lives work. We discussed the importance of carving out time for each other, whether by scheduling an occasional lunch, sharing a hobby, or setting aside fifteen minutes to chat. That's not always easy! But even a few stolen cell-phone moments of girl talk and a monthly mom's night out can do wonders to keep us on an even keel.

Mid-Life Mom *Secret 9*

"WE SPEND TIME ALONE WITH GOD."

Sometimes in the midst of our busy schedules, it's difficult to focus on the number-one relationship in our lives: the one with Jesus Christ. Who can focus on Bible study with the kids clamoring for attention every minute? How can we possibly spend time in prayer when what we really need is a few more hours of sleep?

Well, I'm sorry to be the one to break the bad news, but the Lord doesn't grant any special dispensation for mothers, freeing us from the obligation to spend time in His Word and in conversation with Him. In fact, as desperate as our kids might seem for our attention, God wants our attention even more.

Now, I know there are countless books and devotionals out there to help you on your spiritual path. I'm not going to tell you how to spend your daily quiet time or how to structure your Bible reading. The main thing I want to get across is: Just do it! Whenever I am so frantic that I feel I can't possibly spare an extra ten minutes for the Lord, things just stay frantic and I can never seem to get on top of it. But when I finally break down, admitting my own insufficiency, and carve out a few minutes from my schedule each day to talk with the Lord and read some of His Word, I can't help but notice a difference. Sometimes it's a sense of the peace that passes understanding (see Philippians 4:7), and other times it's more concrete, like renewed energy or a solution to a problem. At the very least, I stay connected with God and I'm more apt to feel His presence throughout my day.

I heard this illustration a long time ago—I can't remember where, and if it appears in a book somewhere, my apologies to the writer—but it goes like this: Imagine you're in a room writing a book, using a typewriter. The hundred pages you've already written (and failed to put page numbers on—go figure) are stacked up on the desk. Suddenly a huge gust of wind comes in the window and starts blowing your papers all over the room. Now you're dashing wildly around the room, grabbing and smacking at papers, desperately trying to keep them in order and stop them from flying out the window. You're so busy snatching at pages you fail to see that if you would just stop your flailing for a moment, you could solve the problem: Shut the window! But of course, shutting the window means you'll have to stop grabbing and snatching for a moment, and that's scary, because what if something gets away?

Taking time out with Jesus is the same as shutting the window. Yes, you'll have to stop all your frenetic activity for a few minutes, and you're terrified that if you stop, everything will fall apart. But that little break could be the key to stopping all the pieces of your life from flying everywhere. The sense of peace that begins to infuse your spirit can make the frantic moments of your day so much easier to handle. The bottom line is this: Focusing on our relationship with God centers us in what's most important, giving us the solid foundation necessary to provide a secure environment for our children.

Mid-Life Mom *Secret 8*

"OUR FAMILIES ARE OUR TOP PRIORITY."

Clearly, one of the hallmarks of mid-life motherhood is an active, busy life. But even with so many people and activities competing for our attention, it's plain to most of us that our families are the top dogs in our lives, second only to our relationship with God. Still, it's one thing to say it, but another thing altogether to actually live it. Many of us have had the experience of paying lip service to the importance of family but spreading ourselves so thin that our family basically gets the leftovers. My group of friends thought it was interesting to note that no matter what else was going on in life, the times when things seemed to be "clicking" were the times when we really put our families first. My friend Susan explained, "When I put my children first, I have no questions as to if I'm doing the right thing for my family." During times when something else is taking up our time—employment, church activities, volunteer work—there seems to be a nagging feeling that things just aren't right.

All the moms in my brunch bunch had careers prior to having children, and many of my friends still maintain their professional lives to some extent now that they have families. But to make our lives really work, we all agreed we had to reorder the importance of work. As mid-life mom Robbie put it, "One good thing for mid-life moms is that many of us have had our careers. Knowing what the world is like out there tends to make us more satisfied with life right here at home. It's easy to fantasize and glorify the working world if you've never been there."

There are times when the children need to come first, times when the marriage relationship needs to come first, and times when the needs of one family member are most urgent. But we all agreed that the love of family and making family a lifelong priority are the secrets to making mid-life happy.

Mid-Life Mom *Secret 7*

"WE HAVE MORE WISDOM."

Okay, not that we're trying to toot our own horns or anything, but the obvious corollary to being older is being wiser. Do we always feel wise? As my daughter would say—"Not!" Years ago, I remember looking at ladies in their forties and thinking how smart and spiritual they must be. Most days, I feel neither smart nor spiritual, and all I can think is, *How in the world did I get to be forty when I still feel eighteen?*

But if we don't exactly feel like wisdom herself, just think how much different parenting would have been if we were only twenty-five. We appreciate our mid-life motherhood more when we realize the benefits of our years. Linda relates, "I'm smarter than I was in my twenties. I cook better, I make better decisions, I consider more options." Mid-life mom Becky confirms, "I've had the opportunity to grow up and find my way, and feel much better prepared to parent from a more mature place in my life. I feel I have far more to offer a child in my thirties and forties than I would have in my twenties."

That extra growing-up period provides a résumé of experiences we can bring to our parenting. Kelly says, "I'm glad I had the opportunity to travel, and time to develop my marriage relationship for years before I had children."

The wisdom of years also brings with it a stronger sense of stability. Julie explains, "I don't question my life like I did when I was younger. I'm not coping with being a mom and trying to find out who I am at the same time. I know who I am."

Mid-Life Mom *Secret 6*

"WE HAVE MORE PATIENCE."

When asked, "What's the best thing about being an older mother?" Becky says, "My capacity for patience has grown exponentially in the decades since I was twenty." Rochelle answers, "I have greater patience and a better understanding of myself and the world around me." Most mid-life moms list "more patience" as one of the best things about being an older mother. I have to laugh, because I know for a fact that sometimes we don't have much patience at all! Nevertheless, we know that we have more patience than we had fifteen years ago—a huge benefit of mothering at mid-life.

How did we develop this increased patience? As Robbie explains, "Waiting a very long time for a family made me more appreciative and better able to see what's important . . . which battles to pick and what's realistic to expect from our children." Our lack of patience usually stems from the little things—the thirteenth spilled-milk in a week, the excruciating slowness of a four-year-old getting herself dressed. Then sometimes it's the bigger things—how long could it possibly take to potty train a child?! Why can't my five-year-old stop sucking his thumb? As mid-life moms, we're more aware of the fleetingness of childhood (see Secret 5), which increases our ability to put everything in perspective and let our kids be kids.

The dictionary defines patience as "bearing pains or trials calmly or without complaint."[1] So what we're saying here is: Mothering at mid-life is still a demanding, exhausting job. But at our advanced age, we've learned how to do it without (as much) whining.

Of course, patience springs directly from that other secret of mid-life moms: wisdom. Proverbs 19:11 tells us, "A man's wisdom gives him patience." As we mature as women and mature in Christ, our patience increases. We also know that patience is part of the fruit of the Spirit (see Galatians 5:22). This means that the more we are in tune with God and His will for our lives, hopefully the more patience we'll have. (I'm not making any promises, however. Personally, I have zero patience for television commercials, telemarketers, or anyone who cuts me off on the freeway.)

Mid-Life Mom *Secret 5*

"WE TREASURE EVERY MOMENT MORE FULLY."

Funny thing about age—it makes you aware of the passage of time. My brunch bunch came to the conclusion that we value the time we have with our children more than we probably would have in our twenties. My friend Catherine says, "The best thing about being a mid-life mom is that you appreciate your children more." Becky agrees, "As an older mom, I think I am more prone to treasuring every moment of parenthood—being much more aware of time passing so quickly and wanting to savor the entire experience."

Linda offers, "I think younger parents might not always realize what a gift children are, especially if they conceived quickly."

The fact that many of us have struggled through infertility, miscarriage, or simply longed for children for decades makes us feel all the more grateful for our children. Robbie, who adopted after years of infertility, says, "Some of us who had to wait a very long time to be a family are really appreciative to finally be the family we had dreamed of." And Julie echoes the sentiments on all our hearts: "Having children is the greatest gift God has given us!" Perhaps the fact that we had to wait for children is a gift in itself, teaching us to treasure them all the more.

Of course, treasuring every moment applies to the whole spectrum of our lives, not just our children. As we become aware of our mortality, we realize "this is it"—our one and only chance at this life. Things might not be as rosy as we'd like, but we'd better savor the days because there's no going backward. King Solomon tells us: "Seize life! Eat bread with gusto, Drink wine with a robust heart. Oh yes—God takes pleasure in *your* pleasure! . . . Each day is God's gift. . . . Make the most of each one!" (Ecclesiastes 9:7-10, MSG). God doesn't want us to pretend things are always fantastic, but He does want us to appreciate His gifts, including our lives and our families. As mid-life moms, we're most successful when we focus on the wonder of these gifts and cherish each day we're privileged to enjoy in the company of our children.

Mid-Life Mom *Secret 4*

"WE KNOW HOW TO NURTURE OURSELVES."

Everyone in my brunch bunch admitted to having difficulty making time for things we enjoy doing. Juggling the tasks of cooking dinner, cleaning the house, helping with homework, keeping up with a job or business, running to activities all over town, and chasing after children leave us with little "me" time. In fact, I think women's magazines try to capitalize on this dilemma, making it seem even bigger than it is.

They're forever telling us to take a bubble bath or curl up in a hammock with a good book. I've always thought those were kind of shallow suggestions, and I still don't think they're really helpful. The good news is that many of my mid-life friends have this one figured out. The happiest mid-life moms I know have told me their secrets: 1. In the words of Sheryl Crow, "It's not having what you want, it's wanting what you got,"[2] and 2. Know what you need and give it to yourself.

Now, either you know what I mean and you're nodding in agreement or you're ready to scream at me and throw the book across the room. If you're the latter, please don't fling the book! (Remember what you tell your children: "Books are our *friends*.") Let me explain.

We're all frustrated by not having enough "me" time. But I like the way one mid-life mom put it: "I consider everything I do in my life as being for *me*. Cleaning my house (I like it clean), taking care of my daughter (that nourishes me), working at my job (I like the job and I like the money), focusing on my husband (my relationship with him definitely helps me)."

I may not always be able to have such a positive attitude, but if I don't choose to enjoy the details of my everyday existence, who am I cheating but myself? "We all need time to refuel, regroup, and relax," says my friend Holly.

Solomon's pragmatic advice in Ecclesiastes 9:9 really strikes a chord: "Relish life . . . each and every day. . . . Each day is God's gift. . . . Make the most of each one!" (MSG). Maybe it's just a matter of looking at all the elements of our lives from a different perspective. We can make a decision to stop the whining and appreciate the fullness of our lives.

When a good attitude simply isn't enough, I have finally grown to the point of being able to give myself permission to do what truly nourishes me. Some of my friends report they *never* take time out for themselves—out of guilt, or maybe fear of unfolded laundry sitting in the basket too long. If you're one of those, get over it, girl! Your to-do list is never going to be done, so you might as well take a break!

My morning walks with Ladies on Track are a big part of my "me" time. Sometimes I'm refreshed by a weekend excursion with my family or a monthly mom's night out. My friend Rochelle says, "I have learned over the past couple of years to allow myself to have some time alone. Sometimes this entails leaving work early and going to a movie by myself." Another one of my girlfriends has been known to send her family away so she could spend time meditating and praying in the comfort of her own home. Mid-life mom Julie gets nourished by sharing physical activities with her three sons— mountain biking, skiing, and hiking. Becky is more pragmatic, accepting that personal hobbies can wait for later in life. For now, she finds fulfillment sharing preschool games and playdates with her daughter.

The bottom line is, at our age we need to be done with the whining about "me" time. We have to take care of our needs, constantly relying on God's provision, so that we can be our best for our families. If we don't make the effort to give ourselves what we need, nobody else will either—and we'll have no one to blame but ourselves.

Mid-Life Mom *Secret 3*

"WE DON'T WORRY ABOUT AGING."

Okay, maybe I'm being a little less than honest to imply we *never* worry about getting older. Of course we do—we're human, and we know our days are numbered. For women, there's still a stigma to being old that many of us are trying to get over. As one of my brunch buddies said, "I don't want my kids to think I look too old for a mom when they're in their teens." Another admitted, "I'm sensitive about my age being known." And as I previously mentioned, my own fortieth was no emotional picnic.

But as mid-life moms, we have a clear advantage, because as Becky says, "If anything helps to keep you young, children do!" Other women in their forties have older children and are forced to face the demons of age head-on as their little chicks begin to leave the nest for college. Now *that* would make me feel old! I'm happy to put off that feeling and enjoy my kids while they're still smaller than I am.

In spite of the normal worries about aging, the most contented mid-life moms say their secret is refusing to waste any energy fretting about getting old. After all, it completely beats the alternative! (Right?) While the milestone birthdays like thirty-five, forty, and fifty can take us by surprise in the psychological wallop they pack, we have to remember to focus on today. In a (very) loose paraphrase of Jesus, "Do not worry about support hose, Depends, or varicose veins. . . . Who of you by worrying can add a single hour to your life?" (see Luke 12:22-26). So when it comes to aging, we're at our best when we follow the advice of Jesus: Don't worry about it.

Mid-Life Mom *Secret 2*

"We think young."

Have you ever heard your grandmother say, "Excuse me, I was having a senior moment!"? Worse yet, have you heard one of your friends say that? They're joking, I know, but it's a classic example of "thinking old." The mid-life mom secret of thinking young is related to Secret 3 (Don't worry about aging), but it's much more proactive. Not only do we refuse to worry about it, we consciously train our minds to think in a youthful way.

My girlfriend had a reminder of this recently when her husband bought her a new mountain bike. Now, when I think "mountain bike" I think of a cool bike with nice fat tires, to ride on the bike trail on Sunday afternoon. And when I think "bike trail," I think paved and flat. My girlfriend was the same way, so when her husband told her they were going mountain biking, as in up and down a mountain, she said no way. She insisted she was perfectly content on the bike trail. Well, the happy couple got into a protracted argument, with the husband accusing his wife of trying too hard to limit herself. My girlfriend made the mistake of saying, "I'm too old for this!" (She's forty.) At that, her husband nailed her with, "No, you're not too old. You're just out of shape. Don't use your age as an excuse for letting yourself go."

In my house, anyone who said that to me would not be long for this planet. But my friend was shocked into realizing he's right. We can use age as an excuse for any number of things that we simply don't want to do. And when we start playing the age card, guess what happens. We start down that slippery slope from *saying* we're old, to *thinking* we're old, to *acting* old, to *feeling* old.

To finish the story, my girlfriend did go mountain biking with her husband. They were truly in the mountains, and there were times when her heart was beating so fast she thought she would explode. She fell several times and scraped up one elbow pretty badly. But— here's the part I love—it was one of the best dates she's ever had with her husband. It was exhilarating to be doing something so physical, so daring, and so downright youthful—and she's decided to make it a standing weekend date.

Most of my mid-life mom friends have similar stories. We've had to make a deliberate decision to avoid the "old" self-talk and thought-processes. Here are a few ways to do this:

- Avoid using the words "senior moment," "I'm too old for this," or "back when I was your age."
- Don't wear plain cotton underwear, sensible shoes, or half-glasses.
- Don't lie about your age.
- Listen to your kids' music (whether it's Raffi, Jump 5, or Toby Mac).
- Shun all jokes about Metamucil, arthritis, and retirement homes.
- Do things that are purely for fun, and maybe a bit crazy: Ride a Harley, learn to water ski, or take up salsa dancing (notice I didn't say clogging or tap dancing).

Mid-Life Mom *Secret 1*

> "WE ACKNOWLEDGE THE HARD PARTS,
> BUT WE DON'T DWELL ON THEM."

Yes, this is the number-one secret of mid-life moms. For maximum contentment and a good shot at making it all work, we don't pretend the hard parts aren't there. We just choose to find solutions as swiftly as possible and move on. We really try to minimize the stress and worry in our lives—an idea reflected in several of the other Top Ten Secrets.

My brunch bunch wasn't immune to the challenges of mid-life mothering, although one guest announced that her life had turned out exactly how she had planned, at which point I smacked her. (Okay, I'm kidding!) One woman is dealing with her husband's layoff. Another is worried about saving for both college and retirement at the same time. Several are concerned about looking old to their children's friends. Susie captured the feelings of many when she admitted, "I know I don't have the energy I used to."

The challenges come in many different categories, and the remainder of the book will look at these demanding aspects of being a mid-life mom, which we will tackle them chapter by chapter. Here's what's ahead.

Mid-Life Mania: We'll look at the physical, emotional, and spiritual characteristics of mid-life and how they affect our mothering. Is there such a thing as a mid-life crisis?

From the Boardroom to Barney: When we make the transition from full-time working to motherhood, we face bewildering choices and are suddenly consumed with the quest for balance in our lives.

Time in the Trenches: Time management takes on a whole new meaning when we're trying to take care of a husband, kids, and a home—and sometimes a job on top of it.

Peace in the Process: God can give us peace, even if our lives feel like chaos. How do we tap into that reservoir and portray peace to our families?

Spiritual Supercharge: We'll look at where we are on our own spiritual journey, how to keep it growing, and how we influence the spiritual lives of our children.

Mid-Life Makeover: We're the most beautiful when we're taking care of ourselves—inside and out.

First Comes Love: Even though we're mid-life moms, for those of us who are married, the husband-wife relationship needs to come first.

Go Forth and Multiply: We'll look at infertility, miscarriage, and menopause, and the emotional and physical tolls they take.

The Sandwich Showdown: Taking care of small children and aging parents at the same time is a double whammy that many of us are facing now or soon will. How do we avoid losing our minds or collapsing from exhaustion?

As I hope you'll see from the chapters ahead, mid-life moms face definite challenges, yet I believe we're fully capable of handling them, and even turning them around to our advantage. The current generation of thirty-, forty-, and fifty-something women are a remarkably strong, resilient, and optimistic bunch, as I've learned from hanging out with many of you and talking with countless more. I feel privileged to be among such wonderful company and hope you enjoy this exploration of the life of the mid-life mom as much as I have.

Meditate on These Scriptures

Being confident of this, that he who began a good work in you will carry it on to completion until the day of Christ Jesus.

Philippians 1:6

My son, if you accept my words and store up my commands within you, turning your ear to wisdom and applying your heart to understanding, and if you call out for insight and cry aloud for understanding, and if you look for it as for silver and search for it as for hidden treasure, then you will understand the fear of the LORD and find the knowledge of God.

Proverbs 2:1-5

A Prayer for Today

Heavenly Father,

I thank You for the awesome privilege of being a mother, and I thank You for Your strength and wisdom that gets me through each day. I thank you for the other moms in my life, for the secrets they share and their friendship that makes life so much more enjoyable. Please bless me today as I go about my tasks, helping me to do all things in the name of Your Son Jesus Christ, in whose name I pray.

Amen.

2

Mid-Life Mania

SECRETS OF A SUCCESSFUL MID-LIFE (MOM) CRISIS

My friend, Kelly, is a mother of three. Listen to what happened when she turned forty.

Hindsight is always 20/20, but I guess I should have predicted that my practical joker husband would pull a good one when my big day arrived.

My husband Mike had written strict instructions on the invitations: "Meet in the parking lot of Albertson's. Shhh. Mum's the word." So on a blistering September evening in Texas, the birthday cohorts in crime climbed aboard a graffiti-covered, air condition-challenged school bus Mike had rented. The engine began sputtering and off they lurched on the short drive to kidnap me. Thinking back, they all looked like cast-offs of the Partridge Family heading out for a concert, but hey, they were out for a good time.

From inside the house I heard a horn and music as the rowdy passengers pulled up, whooping and hollering out birthday wishes. At first I shrugged off the noise. Finally I decided to peek out, sort of Gladys Kravitz-style — then I gawked. There was my brother, hanging a huge banner on the side of the bus. "Happy birthday—39 again!" That's when it hit me. At first I just stared, then I experienced a mild hot flash, and finally I burst out with laughter.

I gathered the kids, climbed aboard the birthday bus, and off we chugged to dinner, a rousing send-off into my fourth decade.

Kelly's fortieth birthday was a perfect antidote to feeling old. Meanwhile, I experienced exactly the opposite.

Flipping through photographs one day, my eye landed on one of my daughter Sarah and her father at the Dallas Farmers Market. My husband Mark had his arm around Sarah, and their candid pose conveyed a sense of love. Next to them stood a woman. I couldn't see her entire face but I noticed heavy smile lines and colored hair. She was an attractive but tired-looking middle-aged woman. Who was she? Did she know Mark and Sarah? She looked familiar but I just couldn't place her until I asked Mark who she was.

The mystery woman I didn't recognize was *me*. I was stunned. I didn't even recognize myself. That shot was a picture of real mid-life—a time when many of us start going through so many changes, we barely recognize ourselves. And I don't just mean lines on our faces—I mean heavy-duty mental and spiritual transformation.

When I set out to write this chapter, I was going to call it, "Mid-Life Is Not a Crisis." (Ever the optimist and wanting to be different, I was trying to give this whole mid-life thing a new spin.) But guess what? I was wrong! Mid-life is most definitely a crisis of major proportions, and I am talking about *crisis* in the truest Webster's sense of the word. Get this: A crisis is defined as a "turning point for better or worse," or an "emotionally significant event," or "a crucial time . . . in which a decisive change is impending."[1] Now, *that* is what mid-life is all about!

My research in the attempt to define mid-life, both for this book and to get a handle on what was happening to me, turned up a whole slew of excellent books. Every one of them does a great job of reframing our perceptions of mid-life, from this nasty, awful time when we realize it's all downhill from here, to this dynamic, uplifting, growing time in which we learn that we are finally becoming our best selves.

As Barbara Sher puts it, "You're not heading for any kind of decline. In fact, you're about to embark on an amazing new beginning. The era you're entering is so different from your first forty years it's completely justifiable to call it your second life."[2] Her view is echoed by Brenda Poinsett, who believes mid-life is a time when we're "being invited to grow."[3] Christiane Northrup, in her wonderful book *The Wisdom of Menopause*, tells us, "Think of it as a kind of labor pain. What you are trying to give birth to is your new life, which your hormones, your brain and your body have already welcomed and embraced, even though you may not yet be consciously aware of it."[4]

To me, mid-life feels a lot like adolescence. Those teen years may not have been a joyride, but they were necessary to transform us from child to adult. What we didn't know was that we'd have to grow up one more time—and the time is now. Just like adolescence, mid-life can be a time of deep spiritual questioning. *Who is God? Who am I? What is the meaning of life?* We may struggle with these questions throughout life, but they're especially prominent during these two formative stages. In adolescence, we grapple with the need to get a sense of who we are. In mid-life, we give up who we've been up until now, so that we can become what we were meant to be.

How do we know we're going through this? For most of us, the signs are there—we just haven't been taught to recognize them. Have you ever awakened to the thought, *Is this all there is?* Do you find yourself disproportionately irritated at the normal interruptions and disruptions of plans during a typical day? Have you inexplicably fantasized about getting a tummy tuck, a shot of Botox, or a sleek sports car? Or maybe on the brighter side, you're suddenly much more passionate about worship, Bible study, and deepening your relationship with God. Perhaps you're fervently pursuing exciting physical activities, such as hiking, running, or bike racing. Any of these can be signs that you're entering a new era of your life.

Mid-life for women has been identified as a time when we begin to break out of cultural expectations, determine to stop living our lives according to an outdated script, and move toward fulfillment of our deepest dreams and goals. It is often a time to stop catering to everyone else in our lives, and focus more on our own journey. For Christian women, this can be a time of incredible deepening of our relationship with God. Barbara Sher says, "What's coming is a gradual loosening of the hold that culture and biology have on you, and the arrival of your authentic self."[5]

Are you sensing a problem here? I am—and this is the core of the issue for mid-life moms. At the very moment that we're developmentally supposed to be "breaking free," we are in fact more fettered than ever. Our children (and sometimes our husbands) still depend on us. We are on a merry-go-round (childrearing) that won't conveniently stop so that we can have our mid-life crisis. It seems to me that this sets up discord between our "inner" and "outer" lives. Our inner voice is telling us it's time to tend to our own spiritual and emotional needs, but our external lives don't leave much room for that.

Brenda Poinsett's book for over-forty women is called, *What Will I Do with the Rest of My Life?* It's a great book, and I highly recommend it, but at first I was taken aback by the title. With at least eleven years of hands-on motherhood ahead of me, it's never occurred to me to ask that question. That's the difference between mid-life moms and, I guess you would say, the more "traditional" moms who will see an empty nest by their mid-forties. Just like them, we're in mid-life, and may be experiencing the typical inner transformation. Yet, while they are poised on the brink of a new adventure, we're knee deep in one already, and it will be quite awhile before we're ready for another one.

How do we deal with this dichotomy? I think one of the answers lies in the fact that many of us have had careers, traveled, and experienced much that life has to offer, prior to starting a family. Because of this, we can choose to look at motherhood as the latest exciting step in the journey—certainly a phase that entails plenty of personal growth! We can get comfort from the fact that, when compared to women who had their children in their early twenties, we may be ahead of the game when it comes to personal fulfillment. We started the process long before mid-life; right now while our children are young, personal fulfillment will have to be redefined.

Another answer to the call of mid-life is to figure out ways our children can benefit from the changes we're going through. My increased passion for God and devotion to studying His Word will certainly rub off on my daughter. My desire to make every moment count can bring a special vitality to the life of our whole family. But perhaps the most interesting side effect of mid-life mothering is that we can often find ourselves in the middle of transitional turmoil at the same time as our children. Will we use our parallel journey to better understand our children, or will we be so engrossed in our own bewilderment that we're unavailable for the rest of the family?

FACING THE MYSTERY WOMAN

Sarah was starting first grade—a milestone in my book. She's getting older, and that was hard enough to accept. But so am I, and I was feeling just the slightest anxiety about it. Then I got the first clue that perhaps I was a tiny bit older than some of the other first-grade mothers. At the 7:50 A.M. drop-off, my loving daughter mentioned casually, "My new friend's mom is about twenty, I think. But I'm not quite sure, she may be forty and just wears a ton of makeup to make herself look younger."

I smiled, not wearing any makeup at that hour. I did happen to take a good long look at this younger mother. She looked as though she was ready for some sort of makeup event. Perhaps she had a guest spot on *Oprah* that day? I scooted home and grabbed my mascara and cover-up cream. Outward appearances going south was just one of many trials looming on the horizon. The launching of a young life into the world was another.

Not only was I wrestling with my own emotions as an older mother and as a mom launching her daughter into first grade, I knew Sarah had stuff to deal with, too. We shared similar feelings—same song, different verse. My feelings started with knowing a teacher would now have my child longer each day than I would. They intensified when I experienced our home during the day, quiet as an empty tomb. It was a crossroads, perhaps even a little breakdown of some unglamorous sort. Life tumbled down for a few days. My thoughts turned to fearful mid-life muses: Am I just going to be dumped in a pile of middle-agers, soon-to-be-has-beens? Had I made the best decisions with my life? Should I keep freelancing in order to make the necessary sporadic income while being the carpool mom at 3:00 P.M.? What about retirement—was I being responsible? Should I try to get back into the real work force? (As if I had not been working since my entrance into motherhood.) My reading led me to this quote: "My own experience . . . indicates that the ultimate reward for fully participating in the emotions that wash over us at this time is that the struggle is over sooner than it would be if we tried to resist or deny them."[6] I knew I needed to go through this dark tunnel to get to the light.

Meanwhile, Sarah was struggling with newness disease: new school, new friends, new house, new long school hours, and new dreaded homework. She had a bad case of the first-grade blues. Each morning as we pried her from her puffy, pink blankets, she explained how she hated first grade and would be perfectly content to return to those easier days of kindergarten. She was dealing with fear: fear of failure, fear of not being able to accomplish the next task set before her. After taking Sarah to school, I would return home to pray and agonize over her feelings and concerns expressed at the breakfast table. Gradually she became settled into a new routine—kicking and screaming, I might add. Her crisis was conquered.

But what about mine? My journey has more peaks and valleys; it's a more complicated kind of crisis. By definition, it will take me years to get through this mid-life stuff. But life must continue even in the midst of a mid-life crisis. I realized that as Sarah and I face our fears together, we grow toward a stronger relationship. School fears are as real as mid-life fears. Sarah may have wanted to return to those carefree days of preschool, but I also had a past to deal with, and I couldn't figure out if I wanted to return to it, or pretend it never happened.

ACCEPTANCE OF OUR PAST

Like everyone else, I have made some monumental mistakes in my forty-year pilgrimage. Since rewinding is not an option, the next best thing must be acceptance. *Joyful acceptance.*

The apostle Paul talked about "forgetting what is behind and straining toward what is ahead, I press on toward the goal to win the prize for which God has called me heavenward in Christ Jesus" (Philippians 3:13-14). Acceptance of the life we've already lived is crucial to moving forward into the second half of our lives. It is intertwined with trust—knowing deep in our hearts that God knows our past and has plans for our future. If we have any regrets about the past, now is the time to place them at the foot of the cross and let them go.

"Having the courage both to embrace the necessary changes of mid-life and to feel the loss that is associated with those changes is a crucial part of creating a firm foundation for health in the second half of our lives."[7] We might feel like we wasted some of those years; or conversely, we might feel that youth was so exciting, we want to recapture it. Either way, the past has made us who we are today. I've found I need to assess where I've been, accept what I cannot change, and pray for where God wants me to go. A great time of the year to focus on these tasks is on a birthday.

BIRTHDAYS

My fortieth birthday brought thoughts of mortality at the same time Sarah was starting first grade. Mark softened the birthday blow with a surprise weekend in my favorite city, San Francisco. I warned him against any shockers like banners flying behind small aircraft or getting kidnapped for unwanted celebrations. Wise man that he is, he complied.

Birthday biggies like forty or fifty can be fun, yet sobering. We mid-life mothers have mixed feelings as we revel in acquiring wisdom but become nervous as we get closer to eligibility for senior citizen discounts. (I, by the way, plan to run to the nearest Denny's and purchase a Grand Slam breakfast when I turn the big five-0.) For young children, it seems like an eternity before the next birthday arrives. In fact, some families celebrate "half birthdays" just to squelch the never-ending conversation of next year's party—and gift list. But for grown-ups, birthdays are a cake of a different color, topped with trick candles—not so eagerly awaited.

As we tackle the second half of life, we elect to live life positively and full of hope. Suddenly each birthday becomes a day not just to celebrate, but a day to turn our eyes inward—to seek God's vision, reexamine our priorities, and plan our future.

What hopes and dreams accompany the onset of a new year for you? What roadblocks keep you from pursuing your most cherished goals and dreams? As a mid-life mother, this process becomes more poignant. Why? Because not only are you reviewing your own life, you are in the midst of influencing one or more young lives. As someone once said, our children are like Jell-O salads: We want to pour as much good stuff into the mix before it sets up. We must be filled up in order to pour out, so how are we filling our inner selves in order to better serve our family?

Rochelle, my wonderful and smart girlfriend (she has a Ph.D.), has a yellow legal-pad system for assessing the "state of her life" and planning for the future. Here's how it works. Divide the page into six sections. At the top of each section write one of these words: *spiritual, family, emotional, physical, mental, financial.* Thus begins your visual blueprint for finding purpose in each of these areas of life.

Once the columns are made, look at each category. Think about how that part of your life is going. Is it good? Could it be better? What steps do you need to take to make that particular area more pleasing to God? This is the inner work that makes the outer person more at peace. Often we need to take some quiet time to count our blessings, or as the psalmist suggests, "be still and know" that we serve a mighty God who is still on the throne. Scripture tells us that if we are to live wisely, we must learn to balance the time we spend in the fray of everyday life with the time we spend in quiet and calm.

Ecclesiastes 3:1 says, "There is a time for everything." That includes the time we need to spend with our yellow legal pad, our Bible, and our God, looking to see what is good, and making changes that might prove better.

In *The Purpose Driven Life,* pastor Rick Warren writes that "God put each of us on earth for five purposes: to serve, to share, to worship, to grow, to connect. Life is simpler than you realize. God's purpose is what matters. This is what's going to last for eternity."[8]

As we navigate through these sometimes-murky mid-life waters, we can find inspiration in knowing that God has a purpose for us— and it doesn't end just because we're over forty.

The *Top Five Secrets* for a Successful Mid-Life (Mom) Crisis

1. Embrace the idea that yes, you are changing!
2. Use the ups and downs of your journey to help you understand your children better.
3. Don't deny any of the scary mid-life feelings you're having; instead, choose to experience them, and give them up to God in prayer.
4. Take the time to assess your life and your purpose, whether it's on the occasion of your birthday or any other significant time of your choosing.
5. And speaking of birthdays—celebrate! Thank God for the gift of being another year older.

Meditate on These Scriptures

Run in such a way as to get the prize.

1 Corinthians 9:24

"For I know the plans I have for you," declares the LORD, "plans to prosper you and not to harm you, plans to give you hope and a future."

Jeremiah 29:11

A Prayer for Today

Dear Lord,

I need Your wisdom and comfort to guide me through this new era of my life. When I am feeling old, please give me Your perspective on age, because You are timeless. When I question my purpose, help me focus on that purpose to which You have called me. When I am feeling the effects of my mortality, remind me that only You are eternal, and that through Jesus Christ, we are "heirs having the hope of eternal life" (Titus 3:7). I thank you for Your constant presence, and I pray in the name of Jesus Christ.

Amen.

From the Boardroom to Barney

SECRETS FOR KEEPING THE BALANCE

Mary Ann, a new mother at forty-two, talks about experiencing a very definite career change.

> *I admit that my identity came from my career, even if that might seem shallow. I was a senior vice president in charge of thirty-five people, socking money into my investments faster than you could say mutual fund. I worked hard and I felt like I accomplished more before nine A.M. than many executives do before three.*
>
> *Then, at forty-two, I became pregnant. Finally, I was going to join the ranks of motherhood. The first trimester was easy. I* thought, This is a breeze; we should have started this process much earlier and had several little ones. *Later in the pregnancy, though, I developed complications and had to stay in bed. It was rough.*
>
> *But the baby came, and now we're both just fine. However, I've found that my desire to rush back to the boardroom is tempered with the motherhood pull. I guess nothing ever goes according to plan, does it?*

Balance is the buzzword of the mid-life mom. Just the word makes me weary—an overused expression that means getting your act together and keeping it that way. Frankly, most moms laugh out loud when they hear the word! Mid-life mom Julie says, "Family . . . work . . . fitness . . . spirituality . . . there are always ups and downs with balance!" My friend Catherine admits, "I haven't found it yet!"

I think everyone with a family has to deal with balance. (Well, a lot of men never think about it . . . but don't get me started!) Whether you're young or old, you have to integrate the various facets of your life so that they add up to a coherent whole. As we discussed earlier, we mid-life moms typically have very full lives. Whether or not we have a full-time job, we are likely juggling:

- Caring for children
- Paying attention to our husband
- Working in some capacity, volunteer or paid
- Taking care of the home, the cooking, and the shopping
- Keeping ourselves in shape
- Attending to our own personal needs
- Managing a mid-life crisis
- Spending time alone with God and in fellowship with other Christians

Often I look around at other moms who appear to be doing an excellent juggling act, and I wonder, *What in the world is wrong with me?* But in talking with many women, I've discovered that hardly anyone feels as though they have the "balance" thing covered.

Mid-life mom Rochelle explains it this way: "My husband and I have recently been discussing the topic of balance and how we don't feel we're achieving as good a balance as we'd like in our lives. Especially for me—I tend to give it all at my job as a college professor, then come home and give to both of my children completely. After that, there isn't much left for my husband or myself. We women think we have to do it all, and when we can't, we take a nose-dive and beat ourselves up with guilt. Erma Bombeck once remarked about women and guilt, saying that Catholic women are especially prone to it. Well, I'm Baptist, and I know I could rival any good Catholic on this one."

In Rob and Diane Parsons' book *The Sixty Minute Mother*,[1] they dispel one of the most crippling beliefs of our culture: Balancing home and work is just a matter of organization. The Parsons say the heart of this delusion is that any mother worth her salt should be able to cope with raising children, working a full-time job, cooking meals, washing everyone's clothes, helping with homework, and still have energy left. Some of what we are trying to accomplish is just not possible.

Becky relates, "Balance at this point is a complete misnomer. You do the best you can with what you have, every day. It's a matter of priorities. In my case, the needs of my family come first, and there is precious little time to meet personal needs—which truly pale in comparison. In exchange, the hours of playing Candyland, changing diapers, or picking up toys make me a better person than I could ever have hoped to be. The day-to-day balance is supplanted by a life-balance of having this experience of being a mom."

PRIORITIES

Becky wasn't the only mid-life mom who told me that balance is all about priorities. Rachel says that maintaining balance is possible if we "set priorities and stick to them." Linda explains, "I think the key to balance is living your priorities. It's one thing to state your priorities, and yet another to actually live your life according to them. So if you claim your family is your first priority, but are always reducing time spent with them because you can't say no at work, then your work is a higher priority than your family. Actions speak louder than words."

Living our priorities is critical to controlling the stress-o-meter in our lives. When we get in touch with the things that are truly important, our priorities become the compass by which we chart the days of our lives (and keep them from becoming a soap opera by the same name!).

But how do we set our priorities? In his excellent book *Freedom from Tyranny of the Urgent,* Charles Hummel tells us, "There is no blueprint for all Christians in the use of their time, any more than there is for spending their money. God has given us widely differing abilities, amounts of energy, opportunities, responsibilities and personal needs. In that light, instead of comparing yourself to someone else, realistically consider the basic components of what for you is a productive Christian life. Ask God, 'What are your priorities for my life right now?' You can then prayerfully set appropriate personal goals."[2]

SEEK FIRST HIS KINGDOM

I think my girlfriend Holly had it right. When asked, "How do you maintain balance in your life?" she answered, "Keep Christ the focus, and all else seems to fall into place." At first I thought it was a bit simplistic. Biblical—yes! But kind of Pollyannaish, too. However, upon thinking about it, I felt convicted by the Holy Spirit and realized Holly is right.

God does not call us to be jugglers. He *does* hold us responsible for paying attention to His priorities for us. Our spiritual life—our connection with God—is the foundational relationship around which everything else revolves. In her book *Simple Words of Wisdom: 52 Virtues for Every Woman,* Penelope J. Stokes says, "We may be able to juggle a lot of things at once, but we can only hold a few things at a time. Our Lord. Our loved ones. Our inner lives. Our outward calling."[3]

Our time with the Lord determines how we approach everything else in our lives. When we feel off kilter, the first place to look is our relationship with God. On a scale of one to ten, how would you rate your spiritual walk? If it is low and you are trying to achieve balance, start by getting on your knees. Ask God to help you understand what the most important elements of your life are, and commit to Him that you'll try to truly live your priorities. "But seek first his kingdom and his righteousness, and all these things will be given to you as well" (Matthew 6:33).

To remove the barnacles of unbalance, we first seek God. But why is balance such an issue for us in the first place? It seems the number-one cause of balance problems is "work."

Work and Family

To work or not to work is an interesting question in the Christian arena. A couple of years ago I was speaking to a women's group. After the meeting, I stood at the book table selling some of the books I'd brought. A lovely lady came up and began talking with me. She looked me straight in the eyes and said, "No wonder you only have one child—you've been too busy writing books to have another!" First, I was shocked. Then I thought, *Is this lady right?* Although I don't think she meant to offend, her comments hurt. In the midst of trying so hard to be a hands-on mom and still generate income for my family, do I really have to put up with this?

As mid-life moms, we're much more likely than younger mothers to have interrupted a lucrative or long-standing job when we had a child. Many mid-life moms have cultivated a career for ten to twenty years with stock options, peer recognition, retirement benefits, and a momentum to keep in motion. Others may not have been so keen on the corporate ladder, yet we've spent a good deal of time developing an area of interest or expertise. It takes years to build up to a certain level of credibility in any industry, let alone earning potential. Once we've done that, the decision "to work or not" once we start a family can take on epic proportions.

Mid-life mom Becky, who had her first child after more than ten years as a television executive, explains, "I think it is much, much harder later in life to balance parenting and work, simply because it is harder to forego established income. Opportunities to step back into the workplace at a comparable level will be much more limited to a woman in her forties or fifties than a younger woman."

Some of us have been able to walk away from it, while others have kept up with a certain level of work. Whatever the situation, the boardroom-to-Barney trip can be a tough one. Whether we feel like we're making a conscious choice regarding our work, or we realistically have no choice because our situation dictates our decision, most of us experience some degree of anxiety regarding our employment quandary. Nancy London, in her book *Hot Flashes and Warm Bottles*, explains it like this: "Perhaps it's our grass-is-always-greener mentality that lends the notion that any of these choices are stress-free. They're not. All of our choices have their demands and limitations, and they all involve some degree of loss, whether that loss is income and prestige or having someone else see your child's first steps."[4]

It used to be that choices regarding work were limited: Either you worked full-time after taking a maternity leave, or you quit and became a stay-at-home mom. I have plenty of friends in both of these categories. But the last twenty-or-so years have theoretically seen our work options expanding—flextime, job-sharing, telecommuting—and all can help families find balance. Each alternative carries its own special set of hassles—and rewards.

WORKING FROM HOME

In my years since college, I wasn't a hard-driving corporate executive, but I did have an interesting and varied career. After I had Sarah, I started a freelance business—out of financial necessity as well as the desire for a creative outlet. I needed to contribute to our family income and support my habits of Starbucks grandes, dinner out, and an occasional trip to the mall. I can remember my first food-styling job three months after Sarah was born. (What is a food stylist? Someone who glues food and prepares scenery for photos. Duct tape, tweezers, and edible finished products are optional.) I had an important photo shoot that I couldn't turn down, so Mark had to bring Sarah so I could nurse her.

Nursing in the back of a photography studio with a tense mom waiting to prepare her next food shot was not exactly a match made in motherhood heaven for Sarah. As I remember, my first thought was *bowling balls*—yep, that's how I felt. Now stick an extremely small gripper on the side of that, and you have a baby that cannot get her lunch. Relaxing was not really an option for this La Leche dropout, but screaming in real pain was. Finally we got the ball rolling, so to speak, and lunch was served. Fortunately, Mark had a job with flexible hours, but our life was a juggling act and it still is.

The unique challenge of the freelancer, besides nursing on the job, is this: You work, you get paid. You don't work, you don't get paid. Another unique challenge is that all the work comes at once, sort of the "when it rains, it pours" theory. Being a freelancer for seven years has been interesting and not without its stresses, but things are loosening up now that Sarah's in school.

THE MOMMY TRACK

"The Mommy Track" is a term coined almost twenty-five years ago, referring to part-time employment while the mother's children are young. My friend, Christi, kept her feet in both worlds for quite a few years. A finance and accounting manager, Christi went to a 75 percent workload when her daughter, Madalaine, was born. "This enabled me to spend the late afternoons with her each weekday," she said. When her second child, Bryce, was born two years later, she went to half-time, working only three days a week. Then Anna was born two and a half years later, and she quit the Mommy Track completely. "This transition from work to home occurred because I was presented with a greater opportunity. The impact I have on the three young lives of my children, and their potential contributions to society, is so much greater than the impact I could make in the corporate work environment," said Christi, who plans to return to the work force when her children are all school age.

SEQUENCING

Some mothers can financially afford to trade their briefcase for a diaper bag, but they do it only for a brief period. "Sequencing" is the term coined by Arlene Rossen Cardozo in her 1986 book by the same name.[5] It's the notion that mothers take a three- to four-year hiatus from work after the birth of a child to be a stay-at-home mom before reentering the workforce. One such woman, Catherine, now at home with two children, ages two and three, set aside a career in TV journalism.

"I was working as a television reporter with a weekly program that I produced and hosted," says Catherine. "I really liked my job but began to feel the strain. I hated rushing my daughter to the sitter, rushing home to nurse her on time, and feeling like I was constantly beating the clock." Catherine's solution was to leave her job toward the end of her second pregnancy. "It has been a very enriching experience for me," she said. Today Catherine works on a volunteer basis as the public relations director for F.E.M.A.L.E., Formerly Employed Women at the Leading Edge, an organization that supports mothers who take time off from their careers to raise children.

So What's a Girl to Do?

Significant changes in our society have occurred since our mothers toed the childrearing line. First, there has been a dramatic increase in the number of women in the workforce. Sixty percent of women in the United States over the age of sixteen have paid jobs; by 2005 this percentage is projected to rise to over 61 percent. Most of us are working in some form or fashion to earn money.

Our choices, stacked together, build the foundation of our lives. To work outside the home, to work a flexible schedule, to not work for pay—we must make the choice that fits our family, not the expectations of others. Everyone has a unique call by God, and our responsibility is to prayerfully make the best decision we can based on the wisdom He gives us.

Bob Rognlien, a pastor in Torrance, California, said, "I believe the overriding principle of Scripture is that God creates each of us unique and there is not one cookie-cutter pattern that each person and each family is supposed to fit into. Each person, each couple, and each situation is different. The key is to figure out what is the best arrangement for you and your family, given the unique combination of who you are and what your situation is. Often there is no perfect solution, so usually we are trying to figure out the best options and how to deal with the inevitable drawbacks."[6]

As we strive for balance, we must take into account all the facets of our lives. Sometimes we make choices purely based on finances, but we need to consider the full spectrum of our family's needs and desires, being careful not to neglect recreation, fun, and fellowship. The balance comes as we attempt to live in peace with our God, our family, our work, and our circumstances.

The *Top Five Secrets* for Keeping the Balance

1. Ask God, "What are Your priorities for my life right now?"
2. Set your priorities and live by them.
3. Make choices based on all the facets of your family's life—spiritual, financial, recreational, and so on.
4. Avoid comparing with other families.
5. Keep Christ the focus!

Meditate on These Scriptures

But those who hope in the L ORD
will renew their strength.
They will soar on wings like eagles;
they will run and not grow weary,
they will walk and not be faint.

Isaiah 40:31

And whatever you do, whether in word or deed, do it all in the name of the Lord Jesus, giving thanks to God the Father through him.

Colossians 3:17

A Prayer for Today

Lord Jesus,

I confess that in my search for balance, I often neglect to bring You into the picture. I scurry from one task to the next, rarely stopping to ask You for Your help in prioritizing. But I'm asking You now, Lord: What are *Your* priorities for this stage of my life? Help me to understand, so that I may live in a way that is pleasing to You. Guide me, so that I might find a balance between my family, my work, and all my other responsibilities, and that I would always place You first. I praise You for all that You are.

Amen.

Time in the Trenches

SECRETS FOR MANAGING YOUR TIME

Lisa, age forty-two, a mother of two, struggles between efficiency and a sense of insufficiency as she manages her family, her home, and her full-time career.

> *Systematic. Calculated. Even robotic. Those words are often used to describe me. I was taught that a good time manager accomplishes more in the moments. I accomplish a lot. I strive, push, and plan. Honestly, my challenge is just to relax a bit, to stop and smell the roses, but I can't take too long in the process because my "accomplish-meter" begins to move into the red zone.*
>
> *It's been harder after child number two arrived. Sometimes everything just doesn't fit into a nice little box, or a personal digital assistant. When that happens, I spin out of control. How do I lighten up when there's so much to be done?*

Planning ahead was never my specialty. My impulsive nature got me into a real pickle when I decided to attempt a very large task in a very teeny time period.

Sarah had just been diagnosed with asthma. It was scary watching

her struggle to breathe. Since dust seemed to be a culprit, I decided
to wage an anti-dust campaign, against the wishes of my cautious
husband Mark.

My thought process went like this. Carpet harbors dust; dust
causes breathing trouble for Sarah; carpet needs to go. I felt certain
Mark would approve of the finished project. (He couldn't seem to get
past some silly notion about damage to the house's resale value.)

So one day after Sarah was safely at school and Mark was in a
meeting downtown, I began the battle. I had big plans, although I
hadn't done much actual planning. My thought was to rip out that
nasty carpet in her room and use special concrete paint to make the
floor a light blue with big puffy clouds. To make matters a bit more
interesting, at the end of the week we were to have Sarah's seventh
birthday party at our house. I felt certain the floor would be clean and
cute by party time.

Out went every item from Sarah's room, and I began ripping up
the carpet. All went well until I had this huge wad of carpet that I
couldn't budge. As I struggled, my sister-in-law, Susie, called. I
explained my dire dilemma and she drove to the rescue. After much
pulling, tugging, and laughing at ourselves, we got that monstrous
load of beige fuzz out on the front porch. Next we attacked the tack
strips. Now, this was unfortunate because when you pop those tack
strips off the concrete floor, sometimes you also pop out a section of
concrete. However, we felt sure we could find a solution short of hiring a cement truck.

We headed for Home Depot and immediately scoped out the most
knowledgeable-looking (okay, cutest) guy in a bright orange apron.

Did you know they make cement in a squirt tube, like toothpaste? We got everything we needed, and in an hour we were good to go.

Unfortunately, I never considered that I might have to wait a while after I filled the holes until I could mop the floor with this powerful cement cleaning liquid. And that was just the first step.

The bottom line is this "little" project took about seven days. Fill holes, wash, dry, paint, dry, paint second coat, add cute hot pink hearts and squiggles border, wait, dry, paint white clouds, wait, dry, and seal.

I have to admit that as we awaited the unveiling of the new and improved dust-free floor, Mark was not happy. In fact, I do believe this was the most unhappy he had been with me in our entire eleven years of wedded bliss. Downright fuming, you might say. And the party? I pushed all of Sarah's stuff into the office, shut the door to her room, and everything went on in full glory.

Okay, the project was a time-management nightmare, but would you believe we have not had another asthma attack since the removal of the big beige fuzz? Mission accomplished. To commemorate the grand event, Susie made me my very own orange apron, which I will wear proudly when taking on another home-improvement project. Which I'll discuss with Mark beforehand.

And I will take the time to plan.

Hummingbird Heads Anonymous

Time management. Ha! Why in the world would you want to read about it from a self-proclaimed disorganized lady?

Well, at least you know I can relate! I've bought the books, been to seminars, questioned the all-together types, and still come up short tallying my time. Add working from home into the mix of mid-life, young children, elder care, and everything else, and you can have a real trench trauma.

My problem is this: I'm a card-carrying member of Hummingbird Heads Anonymous (HHA), an organization for those who constantly flit from one task to another. Actually, to call HHA an "organization" is misleading, because "disorganization" is a qualification for membership.

Sound familiar? In our defense, we're a fun group. We enjoy lots of laughs, sensational snacks, and great fellowship—sort of a birds-of-a-feather syndrome. Of course, the reason we have so much fun is that we're easy targets for a good interruption. I could have a to-do list a mile long, but call me and ask if I want to meet at the McDonald's Play Place for lunch and I'm there! (Make it Starbucks and I'll drop everything and be there in five minutes.)

So how do you know if you're a Hummingbird Head? Review these ten characteristics. If you answer yes to at least five, welcome to the flock—you've earned your wings!

You may be a Hummingbird Head if . . .
• Your filing system consists of piles of papers.
• Your car has remnants of last week's fast-food meals in the back seat. Okay, let's be honest. Last *year's* fries are probably under the backseat.
• On the way to the store you forget what you were going to buy.
• You own more than five books on the topic of organization.

- You regularly pay late fees for overdue library books and videotapes.
- You have lots of fun but don't accomplish much.
- You send out Christmas cards in March (if at all).
- The birthday brunch you meant to have for your friend in May becomes an autumn tea.
- At this very moment, you have no idea where your car keys are.
- A normal prayer for you goes something like, "Dear Lord, *please* help me to focus—oh look, there's a squirrel!"

I haven't always lived this way. In earlier years, I was a consistent closet cleaner who loved to arrange my dresser drawers, shelves, and bathroom supplies. What happened? I blame pregnancy. I'm certain I lost some organizational genetic material when Sarah came out. Sound plausible?

Well, that's my story and I'm sticking to it.

So how does hummingbird behavior fit in with God's design? To find our answer let's take a closer look at the hummingbird, one of God's magnificent creations. This tiny creature weighs three grams and can rotate its wings 180 degrees—up, down, forward, or backward. Plus, those little wings beat 80 times per second. A resting hummingbird takes 250 breaths per minute. No slacker here! Clearly, God knew what He was doing when He created hummingbirds.

GOD'S SPECIAL GIFTS

Scripture says God is an orderly God. For instance, look at how He created the earth. Genesis 1 and 2 reveal a God who planned, executed the plan, and then rested. Does our God of order demand order from us? Well, if He does, I haven't found the Scripture. Whew! God gives each of us special gifts that enable us to accomplish His goals for His kingdom. However, that does not stop me from feeling incompetent around those who appear to have it all together. (I have it all together, I just can't find it. It's somewhere in my box of stuff to be organized.)

Since doing my research on the fabulous hummingbird, I have decided to be the best Hummingbird Head around, knowing that God has uniquely gifted me for service in His kingdom, just as He has you. The HHA approach to a project may be different, and we may find it hard to light anywhere for more than a few minutes; but rest assured, God has a purpose and a place in His kingdom for us hummingbirds.

I've found that the best way to manage my time is to let God do it. Yep, how's that for delegation? God has a plan for each day. He knows the best use of our time, and sometimes we just have to get out of His way so He can work. That's why I try to remember, each morning during my devotions, to surrender my day to Him. I ask Him to order my day and to reveal His priorities to me. Then I try to stay attentive to what He tells me.

Nevertheless, it probably wouldn't hurt Hummingbird Heads to learn a few new tricks. After all, the virtuous woman commended in Proverbs 31 obviously passed Organization 101 with flying colors. She would have been a great seminar presenter for the Hummingbird Heads in biblical times, wouldn't she? Doesn't her orderly household sound busy but peaceful? I wonder how this exemplary wife could help us with our time management. Let's take a look at a few of her characteristics:

Verse 10: She is of *noble character*. So I assume she doesn't waste time on worthless pursuits like reality TV or *Oprah* in the afternoon.

Verse 13: She works with *eager hands*. Her enthusiasm helps her complete tasks quickly.

Verse 15: She gets up *while it is still dark*—obviously, a great way to have more hours in the day to get things done. Are you getting enough of a head start on the day?

Verse 15: She has *servant girls*. Aha! Now we're getting somewhere! Servant girls? Okay, even I could stop being a Hummingbird Head and accomplish the needed tasks if I had servant girls. Let's skip this one.

Verse 17: She works *vigorously* and her *arms are strong for her tasks*. She's not lazy, this one! Obviously she keeps herself in shape. Perhaps if we're in great physical shape, we'll have more energy and be able to use our time more productively, without pooping out.

Verse 20: She *opens her arms to the poor*. She even makes time in her schedule for volunteer work! Perhaps one of the keys is to stop being so selfish with our time. The rewards of "giving it away" might just compensate for the reduced time spent on our own to-do lists.

Verse 27: She *does not eat the bread of idleness*. Does that mean she never takes a break? I don't think so. I think it just means she isn't lazy and doesn't waste time on useless pastimes.

Yes, the Proverbs 31 Woman has it all together. Perhaps she didn't have as many time robbers in her day as we do.

IDENTIFYING TIME ROBBERS

One of the first things we need to do in order to get control of our time is to identify the ways we "waste" our time. Here are some of my common time robbers:

- Mid-day phone calls when I should have delayed the conversation
- Hovering over e-mail and then checking it again just in case something important came in
- Surfing the net
- Task hopping, never quite completing anything
- Too many trips to the grocery store and too much time spent figuring out "what's for dinner"
- Too much TV watching in the evening

It's also important to point out some useful activities that we might, in our zealousness to get control of our time, mislabel as time-wasters. Here are some things we need to *keep* on the agenda:

- Playtime with kids
- Dates with husbands and friends
- Exercise time
- Devotional and Bible study time
- A few minutes of "down" time each day for reading or relaxing

GETTING IT ALL TOGETHER

Do you have as many time-management books on your shelf as I do? They can really be helpful—if you put their strategies to work.

Otherwise, they can be time-robbers as much as anything else. I'm going to boil down some of the most common advice in the books— in hopes of saving you a little time!

1. *Schedule your time around your priorities.* Are you getting a small case of déjà vu? The last chapter about keeping your life balanced was all about priorities, but using our time wisely is also a priority issue. When you are too busy to do something, you have made that something a nonpriority in your life. Whenever you are asked to say yes or no to a task, event, or invitation, ask yourself, "How high is this on my priority list?" Ruth Klein, a personal coach, says, "Too often we allow the events of the day to organize us. We forget about organizing the day around our priorities because we put ourselves last."[1]

2. *Minimize electronic interruptions.* We're continually bombarded by technology: cell phones, e-mail, instant messaging, on-demand TV, cable news, even "old-fashioned" pagers. "We haven't developed personal disciplines to shut off this information overload," says time-management expert Jeff Davidson, who believes we're the most distracted generation in the history of time. "When we say we're too busy or don't have time to do something, we're really saying we haven't learned how to proceed in the face of too many choices."[2]

3. *Keep your to-do list reasonable.* Most of us have more things on our list than we'll accomplish in a day—it gives us something to strive for, right? But how do we keep our lists within practical limits? "Don't just ask yourself what you have to do in a day's time. Also ask *how long* will it take to accomplish the task, and *when* you'll do it. If you do not ask those two questions, you will wind up with an unrealistic to-do list," says expert Julie Morgenstern.[3]

4. *Try to complete a task before starting another.* Yeah, right! I have to admit, I never do this. I try to do too much at once, and time gets away from me, turning me into a Hummingbird Head. That's the wrong strategy, says Morgenstern. "When you are trying to concentrate on three different things at once, your productivity goes down, and you feel like you have no time."[4]

5. *Spend time planning ahead.* Morgenstern compares a day's schedule to a closet. If you shove everything into your closet without organizing items, the closet will overflow. But if you pull everything out, group similar items, and arrange everything in an orderly fashion, those items will usually fit. Managing your time is no different. She suggests dividing your life into broad categories, like your work, relationships, finances, self, and spirituality. For each category, create a big-picture goal. Big-picture goals give you a springboard for managing your time. Remember Rochelle, my organized, yellow-legal-pad friend? Well, get out that pad, make your list, and take on the day. Some people like to do a list for the whole week on Sunday afternoon. Others like to spend a few minutes each morning with their list. Whichever you choose, the important thing is to intentionally set aside at least five to fifteen minutes for this task—don't try to do it while driving the carpool!

DOWN TO THE NITTY-GRITTY

We could spend hours talking about the "philosophy" of time management, or discussing the "big picture" time-saving strategies like those above. I don't know about you, but what I really need is tips. I want solid ideas for managing my household in the most efficient way possible. So, I've asked around and as always, my mid-life mom friends have come through. You may not be able to use all of these strategies, but, hopefully, one or two of them will work for you. Herewith, my girlfriends' favorite household time-saving tips:

1. On Sunday night, I lay out everyone's clothes for the entire week.

2. I prepare lunches and breakfasts (as much as possible) in the evening before school days.

3. I keep a large calendar on the kitchen wall and write everyone's activities on it, for all to see.

4. I keep my organizer (or PDA) and a small pad of paper with me at all times and use them constantly.

5. I make monthly dinner menus and grocery shop only once a week.

6. I use my Crock-Pot most weekdays.

7. On the weekends, I prepare several dinners and put them in freezer for the following week.

8. Any time I am making a casserole for dinner, such as lasagna or enchiladas, I make a double recipe and put half in the freezer for another meal.

9. I write down my shopping list in the order of the supermarket layout. I never have to double back!

10. I have a ten-minute cleanup time after dinner each night. The whole family picks up and straightens for just ten minutes; this keeps the house amazingly neat.

11. I have one place for bills and keep them there. I also have two days a month for paying bills (the tenth and the twenty-fifth), and I stick to them!

12. I spend seven minutes each morning cleaning a bathroom. It's amazing how *little* time it takes to swish and wipe the toilet, swab the sink, and polish the mirror.

13. I try to do one load of laundry every day—wash, fold, and put away. With towels and sheets, I can easily find a load for each day, and I don't get behind.

14. I found I needed routines I could stick to. I have a before-bed routine that includes laying out everyone's clothes, preparing for tomorrow's dinner (get food out of freezer), and cleaning the kitchen. My morning rou-

tine includes making the bed, wiping the bathroom, throwing in a load of laundry, and planning for the day.

15. On Sunday, I make sure I have the cash we will all need for the week. I put the kids' lunch money in envelopes labeled for each day.

16. I have large plastic boxes in the family room, labeled for library books and school papers to save. A small Tupperware container sits on the desk labeled "film to be developed."

17. I have a designated place for backpacks (right by the door). Homework belongs in one of two places: on the kitchen table or in the backpack.

18. The kids do their homework at the kitchen table, during which time I stay nearby but not hovering. I use this time for other tasks such as washing dishes, bill paying, menu planning, or scheduling my activities for the week.

19. I have a special "in box" on my kitchen countertop for important school papers that must be read and returned.

20. I assign real chores to my kids and expect them to comply. Five-year-olds can put away toys and place

dirty clothes in the hamper. Nine-year-olds can load a dishwasher, make beds, and water plants. Ages ten and older can do just about anything I can do.

21. I plan ahead for children's dawdling time, trying to be realistic about how much time it takes them to get dressed, brush teeth, eat breakfast, and so on.

Obviously, as mid-life moms, we deal with time management on a daily basis. Whether we have to be at the office at 7:30 A.M. or we spend our days consumed with diapers and nursing babies, it is important that we spend some time thinking about how we spend our time. I hope this chapter has been helpful and maybe even inspirational. (I can't believe some of the creative ideas women come up with!) And if you come up with any time-management tips I've missed, let me know!

The *Top Five Secrets* for Managing Your Time

1. Spend time each morning asking God to order your day, and listen for His answer.
2. Spend the most time on the important tasks, not just the urgent ones.
3. Plan ahead for just about everything. It saves time in the long run.
4. Identify time robbers and minimize them.
5. Take "me" time whenever it presents itself—learn to utilize even a few minutes!

Meditate on These Scriptures

To man belong the plans of the heart,

> but from the LORD comes the reply of the tongue.

Commit to the LORD whatever you do,

> and your plans will succeed.

Proverbs 16:1,3

I know that you can do all things; no plan of yours can be thwarted.

Job 42:2

A Prayer for Today

Heavenly Father,

I thank you for this new day and for all that You have planned for me. I confess that I sometimes get so busy making my own plans that I forget to ask You for Yours. Please forgive me for this, Lord. I surrender my time to You. It is not always easy for me to say, but I desire to spend my time in ways that are pleasing to You. Please give order to my day, helping me to know what is important, and what can be left alone. Show me how to correctly prioritize my family, my work, my million miscellaneous tasks, and *You.* I trust you with my every moment today, Lord.

Amen.

5

Peace in the Process

SECRETS FOR FINDING PEACE

Amy, a forty-seven-year-old mother of two, is searching for the secret of God's peace in the midst of life's chaos.

Peace— what is that? I mean, really. Is this what I signed up for? I run around like a chicken with my head cut off. And now it's summer. What in the world will I do with these kids all summer? How can I find peace in the midst of trying to provide them a meaningful three months off from school?

I want more than anything to pull my children out of the swift whitewater of the school days and guide them into a calm pool. But I must be willing to be fully present with my children— to take time to hear their confidences and to respond from the heart, from a peaceful heart. I want to teach them the value of a deep breath, of a spiritual pause, of rest— if I can take the time to learn it myself.

I've noticed that when I bring myself to a stop, hoping to draw a circle of stillness around me, my kids are drawn into that peaceful place, too. The impact of just a few minutes of quiet attention can be profound, changing the mood of the entire day, restoring equilibrium to a distressed child— and to a frazzled mom as well.

The stresses of life can really get us down and rob us of our peace. What are the things we worry about? How about what *don't* we worry about? Bills, kids, deadlines, housework, what to have for dinner—things can pile up so high that we're no longer getting a good night's sleep, our dentist tells us we're grinding our teeth, and we snap at our husband's slightest infraction.

Pursuing peace becomes a priority at mid-life, when change comes at the speed of light. We experience changes in our parents, changes in our rapidly growing children, changes in our relationships, changes in our own emotions. Just the other day I saw a billboard that read, "Uncertainty is certain. Fear is optional." I would alter that a bit: "Change is inevitable, peace is optional."

The word "peace" makes me think back to summers when I was young. Catching fireflies, late night trips to Dairy Queen, sitting on the screened-in porch listening to the crickets chirp. Summertime, three-day weekends, and holiday breaks can be cues from the calendar to slow down, plop on a porch swing, and sip a tall glass of lemonade. Or lounge by the fireplace with a mug of hot chocolate. School's out, schedules are relaxed, and recreation is the order of the day.

But our need for peace isn't limited to vacation time. Only by slowing down *every day* do we make time for one another. Only by stopping long enough to observe our surroundings can we bring form and meaning to our lives and make the small adjustments needed to stay on course. Only by shutting out all distractions and focusing solely on God can we create the time and space for Him to work in our lives. Our kids need this kind of pause, too. Regular rest for the spirit is needed for their healthy growth, just like sleep, fresh air, and good food. And just as our children depend on us for three meals a day, they also need us to prepare peaceful spaces for them in the midst of their hurts, embarrassments, and the business of growing up.

When we create a haven of security and serenity—be it in a quiet room, by means of a simple ritual, or even in the space of a quick moment—we make room for their little spirits to grow. I do not want Sarah to experience life as a fifty-yard dash from one thing to the next. I don't want her bombarded with noise, information, and media messages—to be pulled along on a current of activity and stimulation. I want her to learn the importance of *being,* and the joy of simply sitting in God's presence. I want to teach her to live in peace, not to be in constant pursuit of it.

The apostle Paul put it perfectly when he said, "Do not be anxious about anything, but in everything, by prayer and petition, with thanksgiving, present your requests to God. And the peace of God, which transcends all understanding, will guard your hearts and your minds in Christ Jesus" (Philippians 4:6-7).

Now I'm no theologian, but my experience is this: Peace is the *one thing* that God always seems to give to me when I ask. Everything can be in chaos, but a few minutes spent humbly confessing and petitioning our Lord never fails to lead to that sense of peace which surpasses all understanding. Many of my mid-life mom friends agree: When asked how they find peace, they each stated that regular time with God is the only way to peace.

GROWTH SPURTS

Sarah's last month of preschool raised all sorts of emotions in me. I was struck by how fast she was growing. Honestly, never have I seen life pass so quickly and visibly. I literally saw time move as her curly hair grew and her delicate fingers lengthened—and in myself, as my "smile lines" deepened.

Now we faced the last summer before kindergarten. This had to be the Best Summer Ever. That's when panic hit. Exactly how would I have time to write, speak, style photos, and tend to our household—all while providing the Best Summer Ever? After all, I was a part-time working mom who actually needed to sleep once in a while.

So, I began to plan: Art camp for this week, Vacation Bible School the next week, another VBS two weeks later, the community pool. Of course, I also must teach her values, pray regularly with her, visit the library once a week, and, oh yes, make homemade popsicles.

Just listing the summer to-dos flat wore me out. After swallowing an aspirin, I reminded myself that this growing girl needs a mom full of peace, a mom who cares and encourages—not one about to collapse under the pressure of providing "the best."

Any of this sound familiar? Do you struggle with expectations that rob you of peace?

THE DANGER OF EXPECTATIONS

I found out the hard way that expectations can be real peace-destroyers. One of my summer goals was that Sarah would learn to swim. As the season approached I connected to my mommy network. A mom told me about a swimming teacher that had taught swimming for twenty-some-odd years. Not only that, she was a child psychologist. Perfect, I thought. I spoke with Miss Kathy and explained Sarah's fears. For Sarah, getting her face wet was huge. The thought of going under water evoked a Titanic-sized terror. Miss Kathy assured me she had seen this before. All would be fine and she would teach Sarah to swim.

We gathered state-of-the-art goggles, a swimsuit cover-up, and fashionable flip-flops, and arrived at Miss Kathy's backyard pool. Parents had instructions to stay in chairs on the porch, a distance away. When it was Sarah's turn to get in the water, she froze and then explained, in a most logical manner, that she simply did not get her face wet.

The next day would prove better, surely. Again, we arrived with gear in hand. I reported to the chairs behind the line, and Sarah joined the children at poolside. I had to assume my semi-stern, it-will-be-okay expression, all the time singing to myself, *peace like a river, and peace like a river.* All the kids lined up. Then it was Sarah's turn. She politely looked at Miss Kathy and once again explained that she was not getting in. Miss Kathy insisted. This went on for several minutes and suddenly Sarah burst into tears and ran to me.

All the way home Sarah explained that she will never go back, and why in the world had I thought to sign her up for lessons? I felt the same way. What were my expectations all about? I realized they had nothing to do with Sarah—they were all about me. And based on what I knew about Sarah, they were completely unrealistic. She will learn, I told myself; we will just keep trying until she does. In fact, I do not even remember how old I was when I first learned to swim. It wasn't until I examined my expectations and let them go that I experienced peace.

OUR COMPLICATED LIVES

Another thing that robs us of our peace is the lack of simplicity in our lives. This is not a new phenomenon. Look at what Anne Morrow Lindbergh wrote back in the 1950s:

> I mean to live a simple life . . . but I do not. I find that my frame of life does not foster simplicity. . . . The life I have chosen as wife and mother entrains a whole caravan of complications. It involves a house in the suburbs and either household drudgery or household help. It involves food and shelter, meals, planning, marketing, bills and making the ends meet in a thousand ways. It involves the butcher, the baker, the candlestick maker but countless other experts to keep my modern house with its modern "simplifications" functioning properly. It involves health, doctors, dentist, appointments, medicine, vitamins, trips to the drugstore. It involves education, spiritual, intellectual, physical, schools, school conferences, car-pools, extra trips for basketball or orchestra practice, tutoring, camps.
>
> It involves clothes, shopping, laundry, cleaning, mending, letting skirts down and sewing buttons on. It involves friends: my husband's, my children's, my own, and endless arrangements to get together; letters, invitations, telephone calls, and transportation hither and yon.

My mind reels with it. What a circus act we women perform every day of our lives. It puts a trapeze artist to shame.[1]

I'm not even going to try to tell you how to simplify your life. There are whole books written about it. But honestly, what would you choose to delete? The elements of our lives we might want to eliminate—illness, housecleaning, parent-teacher conferences—we can't. The things we could get rid of, like ballet lessons and mom's night out, are things we want to keep. I think we are going to have to learn to find peace not by *simplifying* our lives, but right smack in the middle of our busy-ness.

P.E.A.C.E.

So then, how *can* peace become a passion? Through P.E.A.C.E.— Prayer, Expectations, Affirmation, Celebration, and Equipping. This acrostic has helped me learn the secret of practicing peace.

Prayer. I must ask God for peace; I am not a peaceful person by nature. But through the grace of God I can practice peace. We have all seen—or been—one of those moms in the grocery store line at five o'clock gathering the needed supplies for dinner, harried, frustrated, and disgusted with a child's insistent demand for candy or a toy. We know we're in for several more hours of the same stress while dinner is prepared and the evening to-dos are accomplished.

Supermarket chaos is just a daily example. Add a real-life trauma, like serious illness or divorce, and our daily practice of peace becomes as crucial as food. It is those times when we need to ask for the peace that only God can create. Prayer is power.

Expectations. Unmet expectations can peel away our peace. Adjusting our expectations to meet reality gives us a better chance at living a peaceful life. The world's message is *expect more, do more, acquire more.* However, if we have high expectations that never are met, we set ourselves up for disappointment.

My life expectations were quite rosy. They went from rosy to raw reality in the midst of bad circumstances. I had always expected to go to college, work a few years in a successful career, get married, have two children, live a comfortable country-club kind of life, contribute where I could, and thus live happily ever after.

Some of this has happened, but not exactly how I had planned. As we discussed earlier, mid-life is a time for an intermission to recount the past and face the future. My recounting of the past brought me to the realization that God holds the future—and thank goodness for that! Now my expectations flow to my daughter's life in hopes for her personal peace with the power to reach for all God has intended.

We find peace when we center our expectations on God alone. We have assurance to expect the best from God because that is what He promises us. We can expect Him to be faithful; we can expect Him to be truth, hope, and love. We can expect Him to always know what's best for us, and to be sovereign over everything. When our expectations are based firmly in His promises, we can be sure they will be met.

Affirmation. Mark Twain once said, "I can live for two months on a good compliment." If we take Mr. Twain literally, six compliments a year would have kept his emotional love tank at the operational level. One way to express love is to use words that build up. Verbal compliments, or words of appreciation, are powerful communicators of love. They are best expressed in simple, straightforward statements of affirmation.

In Proverbs, Solomon wrote, "The tongue has the power of life and death" (18:21), and "An anxious heart weighs a man down, but a kind word cheers him up" (12:25). As we pursue peace we build each other up. The affirming of another offers that person a place for peace too, so we both win.

Celebration. As we pursue peace we must celebrate along the way—it is a continual journey, not a destination. We don't just arrive one day and say, "Zippity-do-da, I am peaceful—don't anybody touch me or breath heavily or this state I have achieved may go away." Recognizing and celebrating small victories adds joy to the journey. If you do well, jump an emotional hurdle, make it through a swimming lesson, or learn something significant, it is cause to celebrate.

Personally, in the winter, my mini celebrations come in the form of a Starbucks coffee. In the summer they're Super Big Gulps from 7-Eleven. Big spender—no. Small victories—yes. They're little ways I make a regular day special. It is sort of like adding sprinkles to a plain vanilla cupcake.

Equipping. In my ripe old age of forty-one, I love to watch younger women strive to reach their best. It is truly exciting to see teenagers launch into life because they have so much potential, so much of life to live.

I look back to my early twenties and find my zeal for life remarkable. I had lists of things I wanted to accomplish: hot air balloon ride, trip around the world, visit every state in the United States, meet the president, and on and on. Today I still have zeal, I still have dreams, goals, and hopes, but many of my thoughts go toward helping others along their path. It is invigorating to offer assistance to young people as they strive to be all that God created them to be. So many people offered advice, prayers, and assistance to me when I was younger. As a believer I feel it is our privilege as mid-life women to do the same for others.

> Likewise, teach the older women to be reverent in the way they live, not to be slanderers or addicted to much wine, but to teach what is good. Then they can train the younger women to love their husbands and children, to be self-controlled and pure, to be busy at home, to be kind. (Titus 2:3-4)

As older women, we can teach the younger women how to avoid some of the mistakes we may have made. I look at this as passing the baton, each of us running the race with an eternal perspective. Equipping those younger to reach for all of God's blessings is a gift we give to ourselves as well as to others. To equip others offers peace — peace of mind and peace within your spirit.

The PEACE acrostic offers some ideas for living in peace. Can peace just happen? No. It must be intentional. It must be pursued. It must be nurtured and protected. That's the secret. So with prayer, expectations, affirmation, celebration, and equipping others we find peace. Finding peace makes for a better mid-life mom. Here are a few more little tips from my mid-life mom friends.

The *Top Five Secrets* for Finding Peace

1. Create times in your car or in your home when every electronic and noise-producing device is shut off. Allow your family to learn to handle quiet and freedom from constant input.

2. Spend time in nature—hiking, biking, boating—anything that connects you with God's creation.

3. Listen to worship music, or any kind of music you find relaxing, rather than talk-radio or TV voices.

4. Stay on top of your responsibilities as best you can. (See chapter 4.) We are all much more peaceful without a hundred undone tasks hanging over our heads.

5. Pray—give all your anxieties to God!

Meditate on these Scriptures

Thou wilt keep him in perfect peace, whose mind is stayed on thee.

Isaiah 26:3 (KJV)

"Peace I leave with you; my peace I give you. I do not give to you as the world gives. Do not let your hearts be troubled and do not be afraid."

John 14:27

A Prayer for Today

Dear Jesus,

You have said, "Come to me, all you who are weary and burdened, and I will give you rest" (Matthew 11:28). I am burdened by so many worries, and I confess that I need Your rest. You are the author of peace. I know I won't have peace without spending time with You, and I am thankful that You provide the peace that surpasses understanding when I give my anxieties to you. Lord, my worries today are these: *Tell God what is concerning you right now.* I hand these concerns over to You, and I ask You to give me Your supernatural peace, as well as Your guidance so that I might find solutions. Thank You for being the bearer of our burdens.

Amen.

6

Spiritual Supercharge

SECRETS FOR STAYING SPIRITUALLY CONNECTED

Michelle, a forty-four-year-old new mother, discovered a secret to being a mid-life mother during her pregnancy.

Growing up, I never paid much attention to church stuff. I was a sort of C and E Christian—you know, my family attended at Christmas and Easter. I knew a few of the basic Bible stories, but never did I choose to walk with God.

My spiritual life, though, became center stage toward the end of my pregnancy. I began to think, Here I am past forty and what in the world do I know about mothering? Am I capable of guiding this child who will soon call me Mommy? Guidance? I'm the one who needs guidance—and from solid sources in order to build solid foundations. *The last month prior to my baby's birth was a time for spiritual renewal, prioritizing, and much prayer. Now, I surround myself with mothers I perceive to be doing it right. I need to be around women who can help keep me on track as I navigate mommyhood.*

The birth of a child is a God-ordained miracle, an incredible gift from the Creator. When Sarah was born I felt remarkably close to God because I sensed His presence in the process. Her little life and the responsibility I feel for it consistently forces me, as it did Michelle, to confront my own deepest questions and beliefs.

In the first moments after birth, when we come face-to-face with this diminutive soul entrusted to our care, we do catch a glimpse of God. But is there a way to sustain that spiritual connection as we set about our tasks as parents? How do we hope to nourish our children's souls as they grow up and develop into independent people?

ETERNAL DECISIONS

While I was writing this chapter, our seven-year-old invited Jesus to be Lord of her life. Nothing has ever stopped me in my spiritual tracks quite so completely.

For months Sarah had been asking questions. Do pets go to heaven? Why did God create Osama bin Laden? (I wondered the same thing.) Where is heaven, anyway? How can God be Jesus *and* the Holy Spirit? You know, the simple concepts.

This night was different. Mark and Sarah had gone on an errand. On the way Sarah started really asking questions, which Mark answered. He then asked her if she was ready to ask Jesus into her heart. She said yes. Fortunate for the remainder of Mark's life here on earth, he chose to wait until they arrived back home so the three of us could be together. (I wouldn't have missed this for the world.) We made sure she understood to the best of her ability what she was doing. Then Mark began to pray and Sarah prayed with him, and I cried. That moment is indelibly etched in my memory.

The experience also startled me into a spiritual inventory of sorts. I, too, had made this decision as a young child, but was I living this decision each day? I have to say no. In fact, I had let the muddling through the mundane steal the joy that God intended. Yikes.

MODELING THE SPIRITUAL LIFE

A mother asked her pastor how she should take care of her daughter's spiritual life. The wise minister's answer was simple: "Just take care of your own." Our children learn by observing and imitating. Just as we try to model for them the art of living, we can also model spiritual growth and development when we have our own spiritual affairs in order.

If we demonstrate unconditional love, daily prayer, persistent faith, and adherence to God's laws, we give our children a gift. If we teach them that good deeds and kind words are expressions of the Spirit, we are on track toward living more like Jesus.

Our lives play out like *The Truman Story* to our children. They have their internal video cameras running, picking up our every action and reaction. They rewind, study, critique, and choose their behavior by the actions they see. (No pressure, right?) It is a cliché, but true, that lessons are best caught, not taught. Mid-life mom Linda says, "The concept of God's unconditional love is something I've tried to model for my children. I try to make sure they understand that I always love them, even if I don't like the things they do. The earlier you can get young children to understand this, the more secure they will be."

Here is a poem by Edgar Guest, which speaks volumes about this idea.

I'd Rather See a Sermon

I'd rather see a sermon than hear one any day;
I'd rather one should walk with me than merely tell the way.
The eye's a better pupil and more willing than the ear,
Fine counsel is confusing, but example's always clear;
And the best of all the preachers are the men who live their creeds,
For to see good put in action is what everybody needs.
I soon can learn to do it if you'll let me see it done;
I can watch your hands in action, but your tongue too fast may run.
And the lecture you deliver may be very wise and true,
But I'd rather get my lessons by observing what you do;
For I might misunderstand you and the high advice you give,
But there's no misunderstanding how you act and how you live.
When I see a deed of kindness, I am eager to be kind.
When a weaker brother stumbles and a strong man stays behind
Just to see if he can help him, then the wish grows strong in me
To become as big and thoughtful as I know that friend to be.
And all travelers can witness that the best of guides today
Is not the one who tells them, but the one who shows the way.
One good man teaches many, men believe what they behold;
One deed of kindness noticed is worth forty that are told.
Who stands with men of honor learns to hold his honor dear,
For right living speaks a language which to everyone is clear.
Though an able speaker charms me with his eloquence, I say,
I'd rather see a sermon than to hear one, any day.[1]

Elisa Morgan and Carol Kuykendall, in their book *What Every Child Needs,* ask pertinent questions:

> What will you specifically model to your children? As a mother, will you model spiritual self-care so that your daughter learns that moms have needs too, so she will embrace her own spiritual needs when she is a mom? Will you model strength to your son, standing up for your beliefs and opinions? Will you demonstrate how to handle negative feelings, how to apologize after an offense, how to go on after a mistake, how to respond when no answers to prayer come, how to accept and love yourself unconditionally as God does, how to survive when life has dealt you disaster?[2]

Obviously there is no more important task for moms than guiding our children on their Christian journey. And if we want to set a spiritual standard for our children, we've got to be headed in the right direction ourselves. So, in the midst of our busy mid-life motherhood, exactly how do we stay spiritually supercharged?

It helps to remind ourselves that our walk with our Lord is foundational not only to our parenting, but to everything else as well. We cannot make it through a mid-life crisis, and we won't find balance or keep our priorities straight, unless we're regularly, and deeply, talking to God about it.

Now, you may be one of those moms for whom your spiritual walk is like the air you breathe. You would no more neglect it than neglect to suck in oxygen. (If that's you, please contact me—I have a lot to learn from you!)

...s not where I am. Is it my hurried personality, a busy schedule, a young child, or just plain apathy? It's not that I don't care. I pray; I read the Bible; I attend church. I pray for Sarah's school at Moms In Touch, and Mark and I are in a couples group. Shoot, I've even led several prayer groups for women. So what's the holdup? Anyone writing a book should be a spiritual giant, right? Wrong. For some reason, at this time in my life, I'm constantly in need of a spiritual shot-in-the-arm. Most mid-life moms seem to share this need, so I've gathered a few basic reminders that have helped me stay focused. If you have any of the same spiritual roadblocks that I have, maybe they'll spark some inspiration in you, too.

Make a Decision to Put Christ First

This may sound like a no-brainer. But I've found that our commitment to Christ needs to be renewed every so often, just as a reminder if nothing else. When we take time out to review our time-management strategies or the balance in our lives (see chapters 3 and 4), we need to be constantly holding ourselves accountable to God and His desires for our lives.

A great way to keep our spiritual ball rolling is to set goals. One of my mid-life mom friends sets yearly goals instead of New Year's resolutions, and posts them next to her bed as a constant visual cue. She says, "I write down my personal Bible study goals, such as which books of the Bible I want to explore this year, or how often I want to attend group Bible study. The first year I did this, I simply wanted to finish reading the whole Bible, so I made myself a schedule. Also, I try to set a goal for myself of improving my spiritual disciplines—this year I wanted to learn Scripture meditation and practice it at least once a week. (Not that I've quite lived up to that!) I always write down the length of time per day, or per week, that I feel I need to spend alone with God, and I try to plan ahead for a half-day or all-day spiritual retreat. I find that if I skip this goal-setting process, my spiritual life flounders."

Setting goals is also a good way to evaluate yourself at the end of the year. You can see your lofty goals in writing and honestly assess where you're having trouble, even if your trouble is just in setting unrealistic goals!

Best-selling author and speaker Karol Ladd shares this advice:

When you decide on spiritual goals, you may want to start off broad, and then write down specific strategies. Let's say you want to draw closer to God and deepen your prayer life. Your strategy may be to decide on a time you will set aside to pray and meditate on God's word each day. You may want to add other details, like where you will do this and how long each session will be. How much scripture will you read each day? Other spiritual strategies could include joining a Bible study, volunteering at church, or meeting a friend so you can pray together.[3]

Another good way we affirm that Christ is *literally* first in our lives is to commit to a first-thing-in-the-morning quiet time. I know—we're not all early birds! But I've never yet met a mom who can put off her devotional time until the afternoon or evening—and still actually do it. "Throughout Scripture God encourages us to seek Him early in the morning. Why should seeking the Lord be our first priority each morning? Because God has a plan for our life and He wants to equip us to fulfill that plan. He knows the interruptions and excuses will come to steal our focus away from Him," says Edwina Patterson, author and president of Heart for the Home ministries.

My friend Rochelle relates, "I began to get up earlier every morning during the past year in order to read my Bible and pray through my prayer list. Now, in all honesty, I have started this and, unfortunately, stopped this many times during my lifetime. This year I have really stuck with it more than any other time before. I also have never been more under attack than I have been this year! From this regimen, I've felt rejuvenated and have also had the glorious pleasure of seeing many of my prayer requests answered."

Putting Christ first means making intentional decisions and plans for spending time with Him. At this point in the conversation, many people cry "legalism!" People seem to use the legalism defense to avoid actively planning their spiritual walk. They don't want to practice spiritual disciplines just out of "duty." If you're feeling this way, let me ask you: Do you refuse to change your baby's diaper because it's just your duty? (Legalism!) Do you decline to make dinner for your family because it's your duty? (Legalism!) No, you probably perform those tasks because you love your family, and because it is simply what needs to be done. I think it's the same with our spiritual disciplines: We do them, even if sometimes our heart isn't in them, because we love God and that is what He asks of us. It's that simple: obedience out of love.

PRAY

Throughout this book we've talked about the necessity to integrate prayer into every aspect of our lives. As Christians, we all know to pray. But it never hurts to be reminded again, especially when some mornings we feel dry and can't think of a thing to say to God. Here are some things that have been helpful when I find myself in that situation:

• Use the A-C-T-S formula for prayer. Adoration, Confession, Thanksgiving, Supplication. First, I tell God that I love Him and praise Him. Next, I confess my sins and ask forgiveness. Then, I express gratitude for all my blessings. Last, I ask Him to provide for the needs of my friends and family.

• Pray like King David. Have you ever noticed that many of the Psalms start out with David's heartfelt and agonizing cries to God—then somewhere along the line he switches to praise and thanksgiving? Sometimes it can be very cathartic to fully express your agony to God and put it all on His shoulders and finish with praise and declaration of your love for Him.

• Use a prayer journal. You can write letters to God, make notes on prayer requests and answers, or chronicle your prayer life in whatever way works for you. On days you feel like you can't come up with anything, you can pray the things you wrote on a previous day, or simply look at all the answered prayers and offer thanks.

• Use a daily devotional or prayer book. There are dozens available. While they can't take the place of just opening your heart to God, they can serve as inspiration and motivation.

- Use rare "quiet times" in the day for prayer. My girlfriend says taking a shower triggers her daily confession and forgiveness prayer (the "cleansing" aspect just seems to fit). Folding laundry can remind you to pray silently for your family members as you handle boxers and little socks. Loading the dishwasher is a good time to intercede for friends and family members.
- Pray with your kids. Like Julie says, "Every morning before my children head off to school, we pray together (just a quick little prayer) that our day would be blessed and God would bring us all home safely, and whatever needs or praises we have. I've found that when we do this, we start the day positively and it reflects on all we do."

STUDY YOUR BIBLE

When I get busy, Bible study is usually the first thing out the window. It just seems to take so much time! I rationalize that we go to church each Sunday, we have a great Bible teacher in class—aren't I learning enough?

Elizabeth George, in *A Woman After God's Own Heart,* said there are three stages in Bible reading: The cod-liver-oil stage when you take it like a medicine; the shredded-wheat stage when it's nourishing but dry; and the peaches-and-cream stage when it's consumed with passion and pleasure.[4] One of my mid-life mom friends can relate to this: "I used to read the Bible because I thought I was supposed to. I did it out of duty. But gradually God took my discipline and made it my pleasure. I can't really describe it—except that it's totally a God-thing. Spending time in His Word went from 'reluctant duty' to 'daily bread' without my even noticing."

Mid-life mom Holly says the way she stays spiritually charged is to "stay in a regular Bible study. It has homework and keeps me in the Word every day. If I don't have this to keep me accountable, I don't get into Scripture or have a quiet time. I lose my focus." I agree. One of the best things churches have these days is Bible study with childcare available. A couple hours without kids—the Bible learning is a bonus!

SERVE OTHERS

I think one of the hardest parts of being a mid-life mom is getting out of my selfishness and thinking about others for a change. And yet Jesus said "Love your neighbor as yourself" (Mark 12:31) was one of the two greatest commandments. In fact, He said it was equally important as "Love the Lord your God with all your heart and with all your soul and with all your mind and with all your strength" (Mark 12:30).

Now I know we're not all total slouches when it comes to serving others. Many of us have taken our turn at leading the Brownie troop, organizing the church potluck, making a meal for a new mother, or babysitting our next-door neighbor's kids. Nevertheless, I find myself asking, *Could I be doing more to help those less fortunate than I?* I can think of numerous things I spend more time and energy on than loving my neighbor. Yet as much as I search the Scripture, I can't find a verse that says, *"Decorate your home to impress all your friends"* or

"Work out at the gym three times a week" or even *"Take a Caribbean vacation once a year."* (Not that we really do that!) So I admit, I'm convicted. Does God want us to give up all personal pleasures and spend all extra time and money on the needy? Well, I think it's between each individual and God. The important thing is that we pray for Him to reveal how we can serve Him through serving others.

Make Christianity an Integral Part of Your Daily Life

We have one purpose in life: to glorify God. Often my purpose feels far from that. In John 15 the word *remain* is used eleven times. "Remain in me, and I will remain in you" (verse 4). Remaining in Him means we stay constantly connected. (I have often heard the saying: "If you do not feel close to God, who moved? It wasn't God!")

One thing women are really good at is compartmentalizing. We wear so many hats each day, it's necessary for our mental survival! But we have to guard against compartmentalizing Christ. In order for us to grow in Christlikeness, we need to keep Him in the loop at all times. Some of my mid-life mom friends have shared ways in which they do this:

- I try to pray continually through the day. Even just quick little messages—"thank you" and "help"—keep me connected to Him.
- I listen to worship music, especially in the car.
- I like to tune in to the great preachers on the radio—Chuck Swindoll, John MacArthur, Charles Stanley, and Jack Graham.
- I try to hang out with other Christians—not 100 percent of the

time, but enough to strengthen my walk and have like-minded friends to share with.

• I often try to use discipline moments with my kids as Bible-teaching times. If we're dealing with a particular issue—being kind, for instance—we can look to see what the Bible says about being kind.

PASSING THE BATON

It was a *big* event. Billy Graham, the world's best-known and most loved evangelist, was coming to Texas to proclaim the gospel. Mark and I wanted Sarah to experience Dr. Graham's love of the Bible, as we had each done when we were children.

We left our home two hours before the evening service was to begin. Plenty of time. As we drew closer to Texas Stadium, maybe five miles from the exit, the interstate turned into a parking lot. Dead stop. Eventually we made it to the stadium, parked in the *extremely* remote parking, and hightailed it across a muddy field, up a paved road, over a bridge, and through two closer parking lots.

We were just in time for the gatekeeper to explain that the stadium was closed but we might find a seat in the parking lot overflow section.

Parking lot? How in the world would Sarah experience one of my heroes of the faith in a parking lot? Mark gently reminded me that perhaps nonbelievers should be inside the stadium. So we chose three folding chairs close to the portable potties, faced the big screen, and waited. It was ambience on the asphalt at its finest.

The evening was *made* for Sarah when our pastor, Dr. Jack Graham (no relation), came to the podium to pray. Sarah kept yelling, "that's our pastor, that's our pastor!" Good thing we were outside. All of our folding-chair mates laughed.

Then, with no fanfare, no grand introduction, no nothing, Dr. Billy Graham walked to the podium and 83,000 people stood to their feet offering thunderous applause. The man I saw in a stadium in Memphis over twenty years ago was still worshiping, leading, and making a difference.

Billy Graham offers a simple message with powerful conviction. After seeing him again as an adult, I realized the hymn, "Just As I Am," was perfect for his ministry. In just four days, thousands of people dedicated their lives for something better and now have eternity to look forward to. He was and has been the catalyst of change for generations—just as he is.

Now I had the opportunity to share that with my daughter. Passing the torch of Christianity generation to generation—what a joy! Having the torch to pass, what a blessing. What a wonderful motivation for maintaining my own spiritual health.

The *Top Five Secrets* for Staying Spiritually Connected

1. Make a decision to put Christ first.
2. Pray.
3. Study your Bible.
4. Serve others.
5. Make Christianity integral to your daily life.

Meditate on these Scriptures

Be careful, and watch yourselves closely so that you do not forget the things your eyes have seen or let them slip from your heart as long as you live. Teach them to your children and to their children after them.

Deuteronomy 4:9

Be diligent in these matters; give yourself wholly to them, so that everyone may see your progress.

1 Timothy 4:15

A Prayer for Today

Dear Lord,

My deepest desire is to walk with You. And yet, I often find myself distracted, and believing the lie that "I don't have time." Lord, please forgive me for all the times I leave You out of my plans and dreams. Call to me daily, reminding me that You are always here, always faithful. Draw me close to Yourself, Lord. Speak to me through Your Word, through my interactions with others, and through Your quiet whispers. I long to follow You and to serve You. Please show me how to do this, guiding me each day, and filling me with Your strength and wisdom. In Christ's precious name.

Amen.

Mid-Life Makeover

Secrets for Health and Beauty

Sally, forty-eight, a mother of two, has learned the secret that a peaceful heart, a spirit of kindness, and a genuine love for others transcend all attempts at physical beauty.

I was a beauty queen in college. Yes, beautiful gowns, crowns, and all the amenities bestowed upon those with good looks. I enjoyed my time in the beauty hall of fame. However, outward beauty is fleeting. When the perceived outward beauty began to fade like a pair of comfortable, old jeans, I had to be secure enough with my inward appearance not to sink slowly into depression.

Statistics say my types are the first ones in line at the plastic surgeon's— trying to hold onto some of that outward glow. Fortunately my mother told me years ago, "Sally, you are beautiful on the outside; make sure you are as beautiful on the inside." Her sage advice rings true at this stage in my life, more so than in any other. It is looking at situations through the eyes of Jesus that makes people beautiful.

I suspect at one time or another you've passed a woman walking down the school hall or along the mall and noticed that everybody was looking at her, including you. At second glance, she may not be all that picture-perfectly beautiful. Yet she exudes a certain indescribable something that turns heads. This woman draws attention, not because of some new luscious shade of lipstick or a fashionable outfit. It's her self-assured step, the grace with which she moves her body, the way she holds her head, and her inner glow. The way this woman feels about herself on the inside affects the way she looks on the outside.

Are you this woman? Or are you one of the ones staring (green-eyed, admit it)? What are the components of being an all-around fabulous babe? I think it boils down to three things: health, attitude, and presentation. Are you ready for your mid-life makeover?

HONORING GOD WITH A HEALTHY BODY

After a recent miscarriage, I returned to my gynecologist. He was concerned, and stressed the importance of self-care. "Mrs. Jarrell, pretend you are a fine apple-red Mercedes Benz," he said. (I've always fancied those cars.) "The car on the outside is in perfect condition— no chips, dings, or scratches. You polish that outside with top-quality car products and you look good enough for the showroom floor. But if you neglect to change the oil or keep antifreeze in the radiator, eventually your car will stop functioning," he said.

I liked the idea of being a Mercedes Benz. Then I snapped out of it and went off to pick up some calcium and super vitamins.

The doctor was right on more than one account. First, our insides are much more significant than our outsides, and I am not talking about brains and uteruses here. If we are to be what God created us to be, then our hearts must be well-oiled and pliable. In addition, we must take care of ourselves physically in order to function at our highest level. Our bodies are temples. "Do you not know that your body is a temple of the Holy Spirit, who is in you, whom you have received from God? You are not your own; you were bought with a price. Therefore honor God with your body" (1 Corinthians 6:19-20).

NO MARTYRS ALLOWED

One way to honor God with your body is to keep yourself as healthy as possible, so that you can take care of the family you've been blessed with. Popular television host Dr. Phil McGraw stresses this truth: "You're the only wife and mother your husband and children have. If you take care of yourself, then you have something to give to those two important roles. If you choose instead to be a martyr, if you constantly self-sacrifice and do not take care of yourself, then you may not be there, physically or emotionally, when they need you. To keep from cheating them, you must take care of yourself."[1]

What's one way to take better care of your temple? First, we must decide to make an effort and not succumb to couch-calling urges to watch HGTV while eating onion dip and Fritos.

(Okay, I'm back—those chips and dip were refreshing.) Let's take a look at ways to accomplish our mid-life makeover from the inside out.

FUEL FOR THE JOURNEY

I love muffins, donuts, coffee cake . . . and the list goes on. All that white sugar, white flour, carbohydrate-loaded stuff—yum! Alas, if I want to function at my fullest capacity, I need to limit those deadly treats and make more healthy choices.

This is not news to me, nor is it to you. We know we need to eat well. The *how* of it can be learned from plenty of sources: books, magazines, websites, weekly diet-club meetings, and so on. Let's face it: At mid-life, we know more about nutrition and healthy eating than we ever wanted to know. We read about it in all the popular magazines, hear reports of the latest scientific research, and are bombarded with weight-loss ads day and night. Do you really want me to talk about diet?

Nope. So I'm *not* going to tell you how to eat. What I am going to say is this: Pick a healthy eating plan, and stick with it! You're in mid-life—you can stop all the fad diets and bowing to the latest nutrition guru. Find a style of eating that you think is healthy, that you can maintain over the long haul, and jump in.

If you need to lose weight, pick a sensible (note to SlimFast fans: I said *sensible*) eating plan that won't disrupt your family life too much, and vow to shed pounds slowly. That way you can do it without making your kids totally neurotic about food.

Oh, and one more thing: Stop talking about it already! Really, do your friends need to hear one more time how you wish you could lose that last ten pounds? If you're seriously overweight, are all the fat jokes really going to make it any easier? Most importantly, if you're always moaning about your diet, are your kids going to have a healthy attitude toward food?

Remember Paul's teaching in 1 Corinthians 6:12: "'Everything is permissible for me'—but not everything is beneficial. 'Everything is permissible for me'—but I will not be mastered by anything." A good verse to apply to our eating!

WORK IT, BABY

Near our home is a high school with a lovely track. As I mentioned in chapter 1, each morning several moms walk the track: the Ladies on Track, as we like to call our ragtag bunch. We're all in our early to mid forties; all have young children; all want to stay in shape. As we walk we visit on current issues, school stuff, children's issues, orthodontists, pediatricians, and recipes. Suddenly an hour will have gone by, and not only have we had a good visit, we've had a good workout.

Exercise is another one of those topics we're all experts on. What are the results if we refuse to get our fannies in gear? Well, the midlife bulge, for one thing. Premature aging, for another. Think you're having problems feeling forty? Keep sitting on your behind and you could be feeling seventy when you're only fifty. Says one health guru: "As little as thirty minutes of intelligent exercise each day can retard the aging process by ten years."[2]

Exercise helps the body do three important things: eliminate poisons, increase circulation, and strengthen muscles. But if you're still not convinced, there are two more reasons to don those Reeboks.

The first is endorphins. These chemical buddies in the brain have been found to reduce pain and increase euphoric feelings. Their levels rise after exercise. Says my friend, Christi, a forty-two-year-old mother of three who does marathons: "I have found that I am so hooked on the good feeling obtained from working out that it is far easier to get up and *just do it* than it is to miss out." (She's not getting endorsements from Nike, either.)

Second, and the most important reason to make exercise a part of your life, is that God commands it. Really, you've heard of the eleventh commandment, right? "Thou shalt shake your booty so that you won't get fat." Okay, so I'm making it up. I'm just trying to highlight the fact that we can't do all He has created us to do without taking care of the body He designed.

So, still sitting there? What are you doing? Get up and get moving! I'll still be here when you get back.

Truly, you are unbelievable! But since you're still here, I want to talk a little more about exercise. Quick, name the number-one reason people quit their workout routines. You got it—boredom. "You will always want to vary your routine. If you keep doing the same things over and over you get bored," said Brad Schoenfeld, a certified personal trainer and author of *Look Great Sleeveless.*[3] Hmm, brilliant quote, eh? (I guess we could have figured that out ourselves but I thought it was time for an expert.) The point is, we need to find activities that are somewhat fun and mix it up every once in a while.

Lately a lot of people have been getting into prayerwalking. This can be a great way to solve two daily dilemmas: when to pray and when to exercise. To learn all about it, check out the book *PrayerWalk* by Janet Holm McHenry (WaterBrook).

Remember back in chapter 3 when we talked about balance? We mid-life moms can't afford to be out of balance. We can't focus obsessively on our diet, nor can we ignore it. We can't become exercise fanatics, nor can we be slouch moms. We *can* choose balance in these areas; we *can* choose to look to God for our strength; and we can choose to recalibrate whenever we find ourselves out of sync.

ATTITUDE: HAVING YOUR HEAD ON STRAIGHT

Remember when you were a teenager? "Watch that attitude!" Now I frequently remind our young daughter to beware of a negative attitude. Of course, I need to remind *myself* some days, too! Paul said, "Your attitude should be the same as that of Christ Jesus" (Philippians 2:5).

Writing about women in mid-life, Christiane Northrup says, "Despite what we learn daily about healthy exercise practices, healthy diets, and good medical care, the bottom line is that the most significant way of contributing to our own good health is through the quality of our thought processes."[4] That means our attitude, baby!

Now I'm going to tell you a story, the moral of which is, "Even if you don't have a good attitude, at least act like you do!" Not long after Sarah was born, I was feeling overwhelmed, insecure, and exhausted. To make matters worse, I looked like I felt: haggard. It was a day I had a big meeting for a freelance food-styling job. I tried my very best products to fix my hair and worked diligently on my makeup. I even ironed, something against my religion.

I was running late and needed to get downtown quickly, so I tried to forget about my appearance and focus on a bright attitude. I pushed for the positive. When I arrived at the meeting I forced my biggest smile. The newspaper editor looked at me and said, "What's different? You look terrific."

That taught me an awesome attitude lesson. It was the smile that sealed the deal. One mid-life mom told me, "My mother always said that a woman's best asset was her smile. I found it hard to believe— but as a busy mom, sometimes a smile was the only thing I could manage! I have to admit, it seems to work." My own mom taught me the concept that a smile makes people feel good—taking the focus off of yourself and onto others. So that's my first attitude pointer: Show me those pearly whites!

Now, let's go back to that apple-red Mercedes Benz. For our cars to operate in peak form, we must take good care of them on a regular basis. It's called *maintenance*. When it comes to our attitudes, the same principle applies. We need regular maintenance to keep everything going and flowing as it should. Here is a maintenance checklist to keep your positive attitude in peak form.

ATTITUDE ADJUSTMENT CHECKLIST

Is the view from your windshield clear?

I can't drive my car if I don't have a clear view out the front. So I ask myself, how's the view from in here? What is my attitude as I peer outward from myself? Do I look at others positively, or am I always quick to judge? Do I eagerly look forward to the future, or am I fearful and resigned? Is my view of myself accurate? Have I let my vision of the world become damaged with burnout, fatigue, and boredom?

Anything that mars a clear view is like a bug on the windshield. Let's identify our "bugs" and get about the business of cleaning our windshields.

Are you changing your oil regularly?

Your candy-apple red Mercedes needs an oil change every now and then. Your hormones may be changing, but what about you? I find that every few months I need to shake things up, just to keep life interesting. As soon as I inject something new, I seem to run smoother, just like my car when it comes back from its 30,000-mile servicing. Maybe I switch to a different Bible study. Perhaps, like one mid-life mom I know, I pack up my family and move across the country. I could spend Christmas in Aspen rather than at Mom and Dad's. A little variety spices up the world—otherwise why would people love Baskin-Robbins' 31 flavors? Occasional, planned changes can keep us from becoming dead in our routines.

Are you keeping things clean?

I spend the day carpooling, going to the cleaners, zipping through fast-food drive-ins, and loading and unloading books for speaking engagements. My car is a mess. What's a girl to do? But what a glorious feeling when I pony-up the $13.95 for a car wash, plus a dollar extra for the vanilla-spice scent. When my car is clean, I could just cruise around in it all day!

In the same way, mental clutter robs us of energy and keeps us from feeling our best. When we go rummaging around our brains and bang into nagging worries, old problems, outdated self-images, failures, and fear, it's difficult (if not impossible) to muster up a good attitude about *anything!* Cleaning it up is a matter of confronting it.

We can do this in prayer, in therapy, in a journal, or ideally in some combination of these. Go to the emotional car wash, deposit your coins, and clean that stuff out.

Have you fixed what is broken?

Things wear out from time to time. Parts break or wear out. We hit bumps in the road and our alignment gets askew. Doesn't it drive you crazy to see someone driving around with a taillight out? While we usually try to get our cars serviced on time, we often find it easier to ignore the broken parts in ourselves.

Take time to make a list of your parts that need repairing. It could be a sour attitude, lack of focus, or lack of forgiveness. Maybe you have physical issues: chronic neck pain, a toothache, or migraines. What will it take to address the problem? Think how safe and satisfied you feel when your car comes back newly repaired. How much greater will our attitudes be when we make the effort to create a maintenance plan for our lives?

STRESS REDUCTION

Proper maintenance will help us as we move on down the road. Maintenance is the key to avoiding a breakdown on the side of the highway. One of the most important elements of personal maintenance is controlling our stress. Do you know that stress is one of the worst risks to health? Consider this:

- Forty-three percent of adults suffer adverse health effects from stress.
- Seventy-five to 90 percent of all doctor's office visits are for stress-related ailments and complaints.

• Stress is linked to six of the leading causes of *death*: heart disease, cancer, lung ailments, accidents, cirrhosis of the liver, and suicide.[5]

Did you notice it says causes of *death?* Not just a canker sore, stomach ulcer, or tendency to grind your teeth in the night. Stress is a real killer (not to mention a complexion killer, a marriage killer, and a diet killer). Common advice for reducing stress includes keeping a positive attitude, exercising regularly, and eating properly, all of which we've talked about.

I'm going to give you a huge tip (no extra charge): If you are suffering symptoms of stress (headaches, stiff neck, panic attacks—check out WebMd.com for more), you really need to get into yoga, Pilates, or tai chi. Seriously, these mind-body disciplines are the absolute best stress-relievers, and they make your body feel great. You can choose from hundreds of classes, videos, or books to help you learn. Besides, haven't you been dying to try an exercise called the Downward Facing Dog?

Well, I'm tired of talking about all this health and attitude stuff. Let's get to what's really important—our looks.

FROM MS. ALL-THAT TO MS. FRUMP

I bet Queen Esther in the Old Testament never threw on a pair of sweats and forgot to comb her hair. That lady took an entire year to fix herself up before going to attend a great banquet and visit the king. That's what we need—a year off to primp in an Old Testament spa! Especially true during our forties!

Okay, I realize that's not going to happen. But we are all princesses, children of the King, so shouldn't we present ourselves as such?

B.C. (before child) there was an entirely different me. Okay, perhaps I was a little out of balance, with a bit *too* much attention to my shiny apple-red Mercedes Benz exterior.

I had nails-to-match outfits; facials every other month; legs shaved and slathered with bag balm. (This potion for cow udders works incredibly well on human skin. Caution: Use only when traveling and sleeping alone because it is not exactly fragrant.) I was doing cooking shows that would draw thousands. To arrange the events, I had to go into the town and hold meetings with newspaper advertising staffs and do television interviews. I needed to be *Ms. All-That*, well groomed, well dressed, and together.

Then came A.C. (after child), and I stopped the self-maintenance madness. The car stopped getting shined and polished. Sometimes I think the pendulum has swung way too far the other way: *Ms. Frump*.

Are you in danger of being a mid-life slouch mom? Understandably, outward appearance gets put on the back burner when young children become the priority. Maybe you feel as if you only have time to check on your attitude once in a while, keep the calories at bay, and walk the dog. When can you even think about makeup and wardrobe? The last few years, I've been shocked at how I sometimes go out in public. This is scary to admit, but when I don't have to attend a function or go to a lunch meeting, I do little outward maintenance. Sometimes I even wear the same clothes two days in a row. *What's the point of wearing nice outfits?* I ask myself. *I work from home. My companion during the day is a six-pound, anxiety-*

*ridden poodle. Except for the occasional UPS man. Hmm . . . maybe
I should rethink this.*

My slouch-mom persona seems to have crept in about seven years ago—perhaps I left part of my vanity on the delivery room floor. I make sure Sarah's outward appearance is okay, and then, in a burst of poor time management, throw on a pair of sweats and tennis shoes and scoot. Can you relate?

First of all, maintaining the beauty routine you enjoyed *pre-children* can help you keep hold of your distinct identity. However, it takes a few years to regain the ground you lost when you accepted that bundle of joy they handed to you on delivery day. I have to remind myself that I am a professional mom, and I am always more productive when I apply makeup and dress like a professional. Let's face it, because we are the nurturers, it is up to us to nurture ourselves.

One of my mid-life mom friends swears by a few simple self-maintenance rules that she follows religiously.

1. Make it a habit to get dressed when you first get up—before you even make your coffee, and whether or not you have time for a shower.

2. Do your makeup when you get dressed. If you don't wear makeup, at least brush your hair, wash your face, and put some earrings on. Do not go to the kitchen without doing these two steps! No excuses are acceptable, such as: But I'm going to the gym later! (If so, get dressed in your workout clothes.) But no one is going to see me today! But all I'm doing is cleaning house! It doesn't matter. Establishing a habit of fixing yourself first thing in the morning is crucial to your self-image as a mom. Maybe you're only scrubbing the

toilet, but at least when you see yourself in the bathroom mirror, you'll smile instead of scream.

3. How about this for a rule: No sweats allowed! Okay, maybe after 6:00 P.M., but not during the day. I don't care how comfortable they are! I don't care if you're a freelance writer! Get a couple pairs of jeans and some cute cotton shirts, and make that your new daily wardrobe. You will never again be embarrassed in the supermarket.

This mid-life mom is committed to presenting a "together" picture not only to the world, but to herself as well. What a great way to keep her attitude on track! She says, "Do you think God sees you as frumpy? No, God sees you as *His* beautiful daughter—now go live up to that!"

Many of us have so many roles during the day—from carpool mom to college professor to building engineer. When it comes to our wardrobe, it's not easy to create an all-purpose look that works. It's best to start by asking yourself a few questions. What do I like to wear? What do I feel good in? What fits me? What's in my closet? How much should I spend? What image do I want to convey?

Kim, a mother of three girls and the leader of our school's Moms In Touch, has it together and always looks great. Here is her wardrobe perspective:

"I was in my forties before I felt comfortable and sure of my particular fashion style. I define my style as stylish, not trendy. I choose solids over prints, dark colors over light. I choose clothes that work well with my body type—in other words, whatever will make me look thinnest!" Kim goes on to say that her favorite fashion statements are shoes. "They cost less than most outfits and can add so much to an overall look." Kim shops twice a year. She evaluates her wardrobe each season, then eliminates what no longer works and adds what will go with other items. Pretty good strategy, isn't it?

So, how's that for a mid-life makeover? If nothing else, I hope you're motivated to pay a little attention to *you* for a change. I must go now—my manicurist is waiting.

The *Top Five Secrets* for Mid-Life Health and Beauty

1. It's all in your attitude.
2. No frumps allowed.
3. Exercise is not optional.
4. Pick a diet, stick to it, and shut up about it.
5. You're worth it—so get over it.

Meditate on These Scriptures

Your adornment must not be merely external—braiding the hair, and wearing gold jewelry, or putting on dresses; but let it be the hidden person of the heart, with the imperishable quality of a gentle and quiet spirit, which is precious in the sight of God.

1 Peter 3:3-4, NASB

The king is enthralled by your beauty; honor him, for he is your lord.

Psalm 45:11

A Prayer for Today

Dear Heavenly Father,

I am so blessed, and I thank you for the degree of health and beauty You have given me. Please help me to be a good steward of the gift of my body—this temple in which You dwell. Show me how to care for this temple, both outwardly and inwardly, without becoming too obsessed with it. Please teach me balance, Lord, that I may care for myself and be a blessing to my family and to You.

Amen.

First Comes Love

SECRETS FOR NURTURING YOUR MARRIAGE

Mary Ann, forty-four, a mid-life mother of three, often reminds herself that the secret of her healthy relationship with her husband is "our commitment to God first and then to each other."

" *A long walk down a beautiful beach at sunset is the perfect backdrop for falling in love. Lapping waves, seagulls flying overhead, a gentle breeze wafting through your hair. This is perfect kindling for igniting the fire of love.*

That's how my husband Matt and I began our life together. Then we snapped out of it. Life hit us, with its real problems, real struggles—and there's no beach for miles.

First comes love, and I suppose that's a good thing, because all that comes after that first love tests our commitment. We started with nothing, and often I wonder if we'll end with nothing. We've had a consistent financial strain, barely enough money to make ends meet. It takes its toll.

Marriage is hard; it takes work, persistence, and a tenacious attitude. Will we make it to the finish line? I look to God for those answers, renew my thoughts and vows, and keep at it. "

Maybe you feel as I do, that marriage has two distinct phases: B.C. and A.C. Before Child and After Child. Someday I guess there will be another phase: After Children Leave. The birth of a child alters your entire world, big time. If you're married, your life as a couple changes radically. Remembering to whisper sweet nothings into your chosen one's ear can slip your mind when faced with sleepless nights, endless diapers, work, and chores. The soul mate part of the love that you signed up for takes a back seat to the responsibilities most mid-life moms face. If we're not careful, our significant others can become insignificant strangers in no time flat.

Popular author Vicki Iovine nails it:

> Ironically, one of the biggest challenges to marriage is the fruit of that love fest, children. Mother Nature is so darn conniving, confusing us with a smokescreen of passion and Hallmark poetry to make us believe that having children with our beloved is the ultimate expression of our lifelong commitment. Until that first little cherub comes into your life you forge ahead with your reproductivity like a divine bulldozer, certain that fulfilling your biological imperative can only enhance your romance.[1]

That's where another mid-life secret comes in handy. Mark and I have come to realize that if our relationship is strong, it provides Sarah with a secure foundation and makes us better parents. But keeping that relationship strong comes down to plain hard work.

The good news is that God knows all about the challenges. Marriage is His invention, remember? In Genesis 2:18 God says, "It is not good for the man to be alone. I will make a helper suitable for him." God set up this model of lifetime commitment and relationship between a man and a woman to provide a solid basis for a family. He intended that the fullest and most satisfying expression of two becoming one flesh would be found in the marital covenant. "For this reason a man will leave his father and mother and be united to his wife, and they will become one flesh" (Genesis 2:24).

It all sounds great in theory, but it's the day-to-day, humdrum of life's circumstances that often cause the intended lifetime commitment to lose its pizzazz. Making pizzazz a priority helps the marriage relationship make it over the long haul.

HAPPILY EVER AFTER

No matter how seriously we take our wedding vows, in mid-life we're sure to hit rough going along the matrimonial path. Last week I was talking with a fellow mid-life mom. We were discussing our personal mid-life crisis in the elementary school lunchroom while our daughters played with happy meals. She said her marriage had been rough for a couple of years but that after twenty years of marriage they were making it. "I looked up and realized, this is as good as it gets," she said.

I felt a little sad. What happened to the happily ever after?

Mark and I, too, have had our share of problems. I do not clean house the way his mother did. He finds it difficult to compliment anything I do. Throw in financial concerns, busy schedules, and a demanding child, and suddenly you plunge yourself into mid-life matrimonial mediocrity. Sometimes at the dinner table I find myself wondering, *Where is that funny guy who did all those cute things that made me laugh?* It is easy to understand why people walk away with the hope of finding greener pasture.

Just recently Mark and I decided to seek godly counsel for our relationship. We had a number of questions we wanted help with. How can we better communicate? How can we accept each other's differences—and there are plenty—with the goal of moving on into a union where we both feel fulfilled? What does God want to do with our family? Are we leading Sarah deliberately?

It was a relational spring-cleaning of sorts. Sweep out the bad, strengthen the good, and move on into a more fulfilling life. Love is a choice we make every day. It is taking risks, keeping a sense of humor, communicating, practicing patience and kindness, and much more.

RISK AND RELATIONSHIP

Everyone comes to mid-life with a bundle of experiences, good and bad. Perhaps you're a mid-life mom because you had a false start and are in the midst of a relational do-over. Or perhaps you needed or wanted to wait. For me, nothing was scarier than choosing to remarry after a painful divorce. It was like running my pieced-back-together heart up a flagpole for all to see, hoping that it wouldn't be ripped to shreds by the storms a relationship must weather.

God hates divorce and so do I. Nevertheless, after much uncertainty, lying, and heartbreak, my first marriage failed. I never intended to marry again. It took years to learn to live with what I considered a life-altering mistake. So many of mid-life women find themselves in that spot: forgiven but painstakingly aware of the scars our choices can bring.

Why did I risk this rocky road again? Was it for love, companionship, or the desire for children? Yes. All of the above. First came love, then came marriage, and then came Sarah in the baby carriage. Was it easy? No, it was not easy for either of us. I came with bags in hand, emotional baggage that would have frightened Dr. Phil. Fortunately, our relationship began with friendship and was based on commitment. Friendship and commitment have sustained our relationship to the point of a mid-life marriage.

THE GOOD HUMOR MAN

Mark and I knew each other back when life seemed much simpler. Often my biggest concern centered around which nail polish might best match my chosen outfit for our dinner and movie. He would come by my "happening" duplex all freshly showered and fashionably dressed, then open the door of an immaculate car (no empty coffee cups or donut sacks on the backseat here) and sweep me off to a chic restaurant.

I was attracted to his unique sense of humor. One evening instead of going out on the town Mark invited me to his apartment for dinner. The table was exquisite and the meal was lovely: beef Wellington en croute, garlic new potatoes, fresh field greens tossed with balsamic vinaigrette, julienne strips of carrots, squash, and zucchini; and the grand finale, a four-inch-high cheesecake with fresh berries for dessert.

Glancing into the kitchen, I noticed piles of dirty dishes, the sure sign of a heroic effort in dining preparation. I was impressed, so, true to my nature, the gushing began. As I went on and on about his culinary abilities, a funny grin came over his face. Finally, he burst out laughing and escorted me to the refrigerator. There I found all of the half-empty gourmet take-out containers he had hidden. The dirty pots were just props!

That wasn't the end of his joke, though. I was working and traveling for *Southern Living* magazine, doing cooking shows across the South. Mark decided to write to my boss, a cultured lady who felt it was her mission in life to lecture her staff in the finer points of haute cuisine in some of the South's most exclusive restaurants. Luckily when Mark shared his concern about my inability to discern take-out from home-cooked gourmet, she took it right. I would have been mortified when she read me the letter if I had not been laughing so hard.

Humor in dating is fun, but humor in marriage is vital. You must be able to laugh at yourself and with your partner (I did not say at your partner, even though that is horribly tempting). Often Mark tells me to lighten up. It seems that mid-life has stifled some of my humorous outlooks. The blessing for me is that Mark's outlook seldom gets clouded, so he helps put things in perspective. If humor is missing from your relationship, for goodness sake, go pick up a joke book, add some spice, invite funny people over for dinner, and laugh.

At mid-life most of us have dealt with unplanned, unpleasant, and just plain stinky situations, thus sucking the humor from our radar screens. Snap out of it! So your circumstance rearranged your life. Take a deep breath, look for the silver lining, and press on toward eternity.

THE GLUE OF COMMUNICATION

As our relationship grew, Mark's interesting way of keeping us on the same track took on an unusual twist. One evening he wanted to talk. This was a first for me; usually in past relationships, I would have to initiate *the talk*. Off we went to a beautiful lush park in an exclusive area of Dallas. This experience was my first introduction to what he called *the state of the union.*

Blue chip corporations find it vital to track their well-being and so did the funny, well-dressed man with the clean car, Mark Jarrell. Although I felt awkward when we would discuss where our relationship might lead, I must say it offered comfort knowing his thoughts and intentions.

Anne Morrow Lindbergh said, "Good communication is as stimulating as black coffee, and just as hard to go to sleep after."[2] I totally agree. Sometimes during the mid-life period of the relationship, we have built up resentment. Unresolved marital issues can cause communication to not be as stimulating. This is where forgiveness needs to present itself front and center. We all know that in times of conflict it is easy to pull down that window shade list of how we might have been wronged over the years, thus adding to the strife. If we choose to forgive and focus on why we married our spouse in the first place, perhaps our communication can take on that black coffee effect.

Wedding Day Crucible

I suppose you could say that our wedding was an event made for *The National Enquirer*. It was an extremely warm July day in Texas. (This means your makeup sweats off.) The midmorning ceremony was to be outdoors at the Dallas Arboretum, set in a beautiful gazebo overlooking White Rock Lake. Early that morning I was preparing myself for our wedding. As I applied picture-perfect makeup, mousse, and brand new perfume, my insides began to feel bizarre. I shrugged it off as wedding jitters.

Unfortunately the feelings didn't go away. They intensified to the point that my mother was phoning Mark's mother on our way to the emergency room. This is not the place you want to spend your wedding day. As we were arriving at Baylor hospital, our wedding guests were arriving at the arboretum. I lay in the little room partitioned with a flimsy sheet tied to shower rings watching the clock. I was in great pain, crying a little, moaning a lot. It was 9:15 A.M. We were to be married in 45 minutes. Brunch was to be served at a lovely little restaurant at noon. If the doctor would just hurry up, I could make it.

When the E. R. physician finally arrived, all did not go as I had planned. I had internal hemorrhaging from a cervical biopsy gone bad. The bleeding had intensified and I needed a blood transfusion. Well, this just would not do. After explaining everything I told the doctor all I needed was a shot and I felt sure I would make it through the ceremony. He had the audacity to look at me as though I was nuts. Given the massive amount of blood loss, I suppose the doctor was right, but on my wedding day? They admitted me to the hospital and carted me away, weeping.

If this was an out-of-body experience for me, it was worse for Mark. Right after our seated brunch (yes, they had it without me), Mark showed up with a big hunk of our wedding cake. He looked as white as a hospital sheet. I handed him my I.V.-clad arm and we stared at each other. I knew he was deeply disappointed. I was mortified and sad that he had to endure such a situation. Yet he was kind, gentle, and understanding: character traits that have been a cornerstone of our relationship.

Three weeks later we were married in Mark's family's home. No I.V.s, monitors, or gazebos. That was eleven years ago. We have reached tenure in the mission of matrimony. Tenure is a milestone because in most major companies you are vested, and much more difficult to fire. This is a big deal. Eleven whole years, surviving struggles, adjustments, agitation, and joy. It is a slice of love American style.

THE LANGUAGE OF LOVE

A marriage process blends two families, two sets of emotional baggage, two thought processes, and two very different love languages. Mark has an ability to listen and I have the gift of talking. Love-language expert Gary Chapman says, "If we are to develop an intimate relationship, we need to know each other's desires. If we wish to love each other, we need to know what the other person wants."[3] Mark's love language falls under the "acts of service" category—meaning that he likes things done for him. That's fine and dandy, as long as I remember what act of service I was supposed to do. (If I don't write it down, it won't be remembered. I refer to this as my "creative mind." Mark refers to it differently.)

My love language is affirmation. In my family, you don't compliment once, you repeat it several times for emphasis. Honestly, I am a lot like a puppy getting his head scratched. They want you to keep scratching until the little leg begins to wiggle with glee. It is against Mark's religion to be affirming in the sense I am accustomed to. So you see, our *state of the union* has many opportunities for discussion. Even with a false start, we finally gained momentum and a bit of determination to succeed in our commitment.

INVITING INTIMACY

"Living intimately with another human being is the greatest challenge in the world,"[4] wrote Bill and Lynne Hybels in their marriage book, *Fit to Be Tied.* I could not agree more. It is tough to carve out those times to just be together, to talk, to really listen, and to earnestly understand. When Mark and I dated we could spend hours on the phone just talking. Now we are lucky to review our day with one another.

H. Norman Wright identifies several dimensions of intimacy: emotional, social, intellectual, recreational, and sexual.[5] This last category may be what you think of first when someone mentions "intimacy" in marriage. Of course, it is a crucial part of marriage. In fact, a healthy sexual relationship between parents is healthy for the children. Karen Scalf Linamen suggests that "the bond that is created by sexual intimacy between you and your husband does far more than enhance your relationship alone—it also enriches the lives of your children."[6] Children feel secure when they know that their parents love each other.

Keep Plugging

The second half of life and the second half of marriage—what really works? We are feeling our way through. David and Claudia Arp offer this advice for succeeding till death do us part.

1. Let go of past marital disappointments, forgive each other, and commit to making the rest of your marriage the best.
2. Create a marriage that is partner-focused, not child-focused. (This may have to wait a few years.)
3. Maintain effective communication that allows you to express your deepest feelings, joys, and concerns.
4. Use anger and conflict creatively to build your relationship.
5. Build a deeper friendship and enjoy your spouse.
6. Renew romance and restore a pleasurable sexual relationship.
7. Adjust to changing roles with aging parents and adult children.
8. Evaluate where you are on your spiritual pilgrimage.[7]

James Dobson has said, "It is not enough to make a great start toward a long-term marriage. You will need the determination to keep plugging, even when every fiber in your body longs for (something else). Only then will you make it to the end. But hang in there."

The *Top Five Secrets* for Nurturing Your Marriage

1. Don't expect your marriage to always stay the same.
2. Remember that nurturing your marriage is good for your kids.
3. Keep a sense of humor.
4. Seek counseling if necessary.
5. Don't neglect intimacy.

Meditate on These Scriptures

Now to him who is able to do immeasurably more than all we ask or imagine, according to his power that is at work within us, to him be glory in the church and in Christ Jesus throughout all generations, for ever and ever! Amen.

Ephesians 3:20-21

Love is patient, love is kind. It does not envy, it does not boast, it is not proud. It is not rude, it is not self-seeking, it is not easily angered, it keeps no record of wrongs. Love does not delight in evil but rejoices with the truth. It always protects, always trusts, always hopes, always perseveres.

1 Corinthians 13:4-7

A Prayer for Today

Lord Jesus,

I thank you for the glorious gift and privilege of marriage. I am so grateful for the good times we've had and for the blessing of children. I pray for the wisdom to know what my husband needs and the fortitude to be able to give it to him. I ask for Your strength to keep my marriage going when it's tough and that You would grant me the continuing desire to honor this commitment forever. Please bless our marriage with Your constant presence. In Your precious name I pray.

Amen.

9

Go Forth and Multiply

SECRETS FOR HANDLING REPRODUCTIVE CHALLENGES

Mary Beth, age forty-two, mother of one, struggles with sadness after the loss of her unborn child. She desires for her friends to listen instead of advise.

I know millions of women experience the loss of an unborn child. Even though it is quite sad, everyone seems to expect you to just get on with it . . . you know, life. But the sadness looms. You feel it sometimes when you least expect to; often those times are inconvenient or even embarrassing. It is sadness for the loss of what might have been. I do not look at it as the salvation from something medically awful; I look at it as the loss of great potential. The loss of a sibling for my child, the loss of the joy a baby can bring, the loss of growing my family to what I had always hoped.

I feel the best when my friends don't encourage me to look at the bright side or tell me that we can try again. At mid-life my time for trying is limited. I am helped most by those who listen to my story. Talking about my miscarriage is a release, my way of grieving.

Infertility is the "should, could, hurry up and wait disease." You wait for the test to come back, you wait for the pregnancy

test to turn a positive color, you wait to see if your period will
start. You pray and wait for God's direction as to the next steps
to take. Should we adopt? Should we try a new medicine? Should
we be grateful for what God has already given us?

Eggs. We dye, devil, hide, roll, and boil them. We crack, beat, whip, sauté, and separate them. I love eggs. I eat them scrambled and sprinkled with grated cheese, or fried up in a cast iron skillet with a dash of pepper, or poached and hidden between a flaky croissant. You could call me a bona fide brunch gal.

But those other eggs—the human kind—I never gave much thought. Until mine seemed suddenly to fly the fertility coop. Infertility, miscarriages, uncertainty. It is the scrambled expectations that ruffle the feathers of a couple trying to "be fruitful and multiply." So many questions; so many options. Should we adopt? Should we try invitro? What is the cost of all this scientific assistance? How does God view our assisting Him with our reproductive system? Why does it seem so easy for other families? These are just a few of the questions that swirl around in my brain as I count the days on the calendar, yet one more month.

Infertility is a lonely spot. It can become all-consuming, thus stealing the joy God gives. Children are a gift from God, so why isn't this working? Ultimately it is reassuring to know that God is in control. He holds the future, the eggs in the ovaries, and knows the plans He has for me. You see, that is where the buck stops; that is where I find my peace.

Baby on Board?

The egg toss began almost immediately after Mark and I married. I became pregnant. Good egg, good egg! Yessiree, baby on board. The blood work said, "Definitely with child."

Then, as the excitement of a new life began to build, the sonogram showed what seemed a cruel joke: a sac but no heartbeat. "What?" I exclaimed. "Are you kidding me?" My seasoned ob-gyn assumed his best bedside manner, realizing that he had a hormonal, empty-armed, mid-life mom-wannabe on his hands. Thirteen weeks into an assumed normal pregnancy resulted in a miscarriage, or what the doctor termed a blighted ovum. It was a fast track to the twilight zone. Now you're pregnant, now you're not. Now your eggs work, now they don't. To say the least, my brain felt fried, and it was not sunny side up.

One year later it worked. Good egg! A real-life full-term chickadee we call Sarah. It was exciting at the doctor's office to take a peak inside her petite pool and view the progress of her little body. Each stage of the pregnancy was fascinating. I loved feeling the flutters of movement from the inside out, or watching my pajamas jump and dance when I laid flat on the bed. We were having a genuine Discovery Channel adventure in the comfort of our own home.

Red Flags Flying

My first trip to the gynecologist after Sarah was born was riveting. Everything checked out just fine, but then the discussion turned odd. Dr. Bodden began to ask about our future reproductive plans.

"Reproductively you are considered an older woman," he explained. What was he getting at? Surely he had forgotten he was speaking to an enormously sleep-deprived individual who was still walking like she had ridden a horse from Delaware to Oregon. At this point in our new-parent voyage, Mark and I were still falling asleep at the dinner table because both of us had been up all night—we were not thinking about baby number two.

The good doctor was. He handed me a pile of literature covering the inclement health possibilities looming on the horizon for women over 35. After a few departing words of wisdom, Dr. Bodden signed my chart and went off to his next lady in waiting. Slowly I picked up my things, stuffed the voluminous health literature in my purse, and pushed my stretched-out stomach back into my jeans. Grabbing my bundle of joy, we headed right to the Arby's drive-through for a Big Montana. (Nursing made me as hungry as a horse.)

In our new millenium it has become more common for women to bear healthy children in their forties. In fact, my doctor told me that he delivers healthy babies to healthy mid-life moms regularly. However, doctors must have to take an oath in medical school, promising to send up a red flag when their patients hit a certain age. My particular red flag has been waving high for years.

Womb with a View—Vacancy

Then, in the blink of an eye, years passed. Never does time go as quickly as it does with a child. By now Mark and I had begun to hope for a second child. I began to dread the yearly appointment with my personal Father Time figure, the gynecologist. With each visit my biological clock ticked louder and louder. I'm sure it could be heard in the exam room next door. As I reached the end of my third decade, our thoughts of baby number two turned to constant concern. The ovaries appeared closed for business.

Doreen Nagle, in her book, *But I Don't Feel Too Old to Be a Mommy,* writes, "Women seem to be misled and/or ignorant of their fertility timeline. Many women think they'll get pregnant whenever they choose just because they feel they are ready to be a mother. This thinking severely underestimates the truth. Seventy-five percent of women over thirty-five experience fertility problems in some form or fashion."[1]

"The saying, 'It's never too late' was not meant for women who wait too long to get pregnant," says obstetrical psychologist Dr. Roxanne Head.[2]

Had Mark and I waited too long? All those diaper and juice ads on TV could bring me to real tears. Perhaps if I had not always assumed I would have two children and live a comfortable life, this would not have been so upsetting. Expectations can rob your life. Comparison to others who "seem" to have a smooth and easy life can steal your happiness. How does one *unexpect* when their heart wants desperately to be expecting? It has to be a God thing or you shrivel into bitterness.

WOMB WITH A VIEW — REMODELING

Was God just saying, "No," or were we supposed to take matters into our own hands? Choosing to take control of our infertility challenges was a difficult decision. We would discuss and discuss our options. Were we playing God? We sought wise counsel. One friend explained it like this, "If your arm was broken, would you have it set?" Sounds logical, but we are talking about another life now. Risks, health concerns, financial implications. Finally, we chose once again to review our options with a medical professional.

We made an appointment with Dr. Bodden, the same guy who delivered Sarah, the same one with the reams of health literature. Mark and I arrived in separate cars, he from work and me from home. In the exam room I donned my lovely pea-green hospital gown, wrapped myself in a crisp sheet, and climbed aboard the table, shaking from the cold—and from nerves. Mark sat in the only chair and grabbed a magazine. I looked around the ice-cold room. The first thing I saw was a simplistic pamphlet on menopause. Hey, they must have looked at my birthday and put us in the hot flash room, not realizing we had come to talk about a baby.

After what seemed like hours, the door opened and in walked Dr. Bodden, or Father Time as we call him. He apologized for the cold room, did his routine stuff, then asked if we had any questions. He must have known something was up because Mark did not normally come with me.

"Doctor, I am forty-one years old, we have tried to have a second child for four years, what are our options?" I asked. I bet he was thinking, *Honey, you should have been in here a long time ago; all the literature says so.*

He was kind, but quite precise. He reviewed options from medications to surrogates. He said if you have been trying this long, more than likely regular medications would not help you. You will have to use the "supercharged fertility routine." In my mind I visualized a '56 Chevy, with the hood up, its battery attached to rusty jumper cables in an effort to jumpstart the engine.

Fertility procedures came with risks, he reminded us. I knew I needed to decide just how serious a walking science project I was willing to be. When the doctor explained a 10 percent chance of multiples I visualized that '56 Chevy full of sextuplets—all in matching outfits, pulling up to the sound studio of "Good Morning America" to retrieve their year's supply of free diapers. No, thank you.

I was not encouraged, even though he peppered his conversation with examples of deliveries to older mothers. "Hey, last week I delivered a fifty-two-year old woman, with twins," he said. "The week before that the lady was forty-four and all went well." I felt old. It seemed as though I was watching someone else navigate a sad situation.

Here's what is really ironic about that cold, discouraging conversation. At that moment I was pregnant. That's right, my forty-one-year-old egg worked, bless its heart. After taking the blood tests needed to review our fertility options, Dr. Bodden called to tell me. "You are just kidding me," I said. But Father Time isn't the teasing kind. I was in shock.

He gave me my marching orders and off I flew to get those folic acid prenatal "horse pill" vitamins. We were finally going to have another baby! Although I was trying to hold back being entirely thrilled, I had this sudden urge to drive my visual picture of fertility, the '56 Chevy, up to a mountaintop and scream—God gave us our miracle!

Unfortunately, we weren't to have a mountaintop experience. Poor little egg gave it its best shot, but it did not make it. The weekend following the news from Dr. Bodden, I thought my body felt funny, but it had been seven years since my last pregnancy and ten years since my last miscarriage. On Saturday evening while we were all watching *Barbie as Rapunzel,* it became quite obvious that our little miracle was gone. Fortunate in one way, I suppose. I could have carried this baby for months and then lost it. But sad all the same. I felt God had been chuckling from heaven as we sat, taking matters into our own hands, in the fertility doctor's office while all the time pregnant. As hormones bounce back and forth with the force of a well-fired pinball, I reflect and look for God's faithfulness. Hey, I know it's there. Somewhere in the midst of my confusion, I just have to find it.

The first verse of Hebrews 11 reminds us that "faith is being sure of what we hope for and certain of what we do not see." How do you push toward faith when your heart is filled with uncertainty? Perhaps you have tried for years to have another child and can't for reasons other than mine. Perhaps you've struggled, too, with how to deal with your loss. It is a painful day-to-day process of seeking God for answers to your questions. I have found that surrounding myself with friends who care and taking time to allow myself to grieve become the ropes for pulling myself out of the sadness.

Faith means abandoning all trust in our own resources. Apart from being wise about health concerns, we have no real control over what our body is doing when it comes to being—or not being—pregnant. All we can truly rely on is faith in a God who is in control. When this miscarriage became imminent, my first thought was, *What could I do to stop this from happening?* Reality shows that there was nothing I could do. It did not matter that we had worked for this for five years. What mattered was that God was, and still is, in control. Who knows what He saved us from? We will never know. Again, we go back to faith. It means relying on things we cannot see—God's promises, provisions, and His concerns for us. It is not just an inner attitude, though. For faith to be present, action is required. Faith proves itself by its obedience to the Lord.

THE END OF AN ERA

Infertility, miscarriage. What other reproductive joys does mid-life have to offer?

Menopause. There, I said it. I still cannot believe I'm knocking on the door of this milestone. When I was younger, I always heard it referred to as "the change." I thought, *What change?* What in the world do women mean when they talk about this stuff? Now I'm starting to see that it's really a big *change,* not just in the fertility department, but in other areas as well.

You see, when I heard the word "menopause" I visualized support hose, girdles, pancake makeup, sensible shoes, and a bona fide AARP membership card. Of course, none of that applies to me. I've no desire to shop for the aforementioned items, and frankly, I doubt I ever will. (Probably a premature announcement on my part, but hey, a girl can dream.)

The textbook definition of menopause is when a woman does not have a period for twelve months. However, I've found that menopause resists simple definition. It is both a journey and a destination. When I did an Internet search, I found lots of drug companies explaining the terrible symptoms as they tried to sell their products for easing the transition.

Derived from the ancient Greek word *men,* meaning month and moon, and *pauein,* meaning to cease, menopause has been called "the change" suggesting both its magnitude and its mystery. More recently, some have attempted to rename it estrogen deficiency disease (this is for the politically correct) or adult onset ovarian failure (this is for the negative at heart). Call it what you want; the way I see it, we stop buying tampons, we can no longer have children naturally, and we endure various and sundry unpleasant side effects along the way.

Hormone Hilda

During one of our many visits to Father Time to discern the likelihood of conception, my doctor did the menopause blood test on me. Yes, if you are in the right age range, you can get a handy blood test to figure out your fate. A good thing, too—we were at a loss to figure out what the heck was going on with me. Hmm, menopause, versus PMS, versus a plain bad mood, versus being upset for having not conceived. Can you tell me how we're supposed to tell the difference between real-life menopause stuff and regular female foibles? My blood test came back "normal"—meaning, I guess, that all my craziness could not be blamed on *the change* (making "plain bad mood" the winner).

Well, my hormones never got the memo about the normal blood test and proceeded to do their own thing, sending me into fits — physical, emotional, and literal on occasion. After one particularly difficult monthly fiasco, I was prescribed medication — more hormones, just what I needed! I couldn't get over the fact that I still felt eighteen inside but was headed like a fast horse to the barn of the dreaded HRT. I dutifully took the estrogen pills, gained five pounds, and had to get new relaxed-fit jeans from The Gap. Still feeling a bit uncertain as to what I was up against, I asked some older moms to fess up and give me a not-so-medical account of what to anticipate. Take a look at the yummy buffet of possibilities:

Hot flashes. You feel a slow rush, especially in your face, and it rises until you wonder if it's really this hot in the room, or is it you? You may sweat, too, meaning you could experience those other menopause symptoms, makeup melt or wet T-shirt. (Who said midlife wasn't sexy?)

Mood swings. As the estrogen swings, so do you. It used to happen in monthly cycles, now you can witness the entire spectrum of your moods in mere minutes.

Bloating or weight gain. This is otherwise known as watching your most comfortable pair of jeans slowly cut off your circulation. You've read the Midol bottle — "temporary water weight gain," they say — but don't be fooled. At this time of life, it may not be so temporary.

Lack of sexual desire. Phew! I've avoided this one so far, but they say it's directly related to hormones. Of course, mid-life moms know it can be even more closely related to chasing a toddler around all day. The only way to know if it's your testosterone level or just your life is to get the blood test.

Decreased periods or heavier periods. Sometimes I wish they would make up their minds, don't you? Alas, it's simply the truth: Some ladies slow down while others speed up. Your cycle can change and be fast, then slow. As my mother told me when I was twelve, always be prepared.

Fatigue. They've got to be kidding, right? A twenty-year-old is tired after chasing kids all day. Add twenty-odd years and hormonal chaos to the mix, and fatigue can become your new daily companion.

Well, those are the physical symptoms, but what does it all mean? It means that over a span of about fifteen years or so, you will have a bunch of crummy symptoms and very strange periods, until your period finally stops altogether. Yes, these symptoms could last a decade and a half!

Take heart. Remember all that stuff way back in chapter 2 about how mid-life is a time of wonderful personal growth for women? Here's where the symptoms of menopause come in handy. Many people think they are really signals from our body, telling us to wake up and smell the coffee. Time is short! Define your goals, dream your dreams, get with the program because there's not much time left. It's time to start being who we were really meant to be. So when you feel a hot flash coming on, just enjoy your deepening wisdom and go change that diaper.

If you want to read an amazing book about menopause and every emotion you ever had, get Christiane Northrup's *The Wisdom of Menopause*. She explains it much better than I do.

HOW BIG IS YOUR GOD?

The Lord may have said, "Be fruitful and increase in number; multiply on the earth and increase upon it" (Genesis 9:7), but it seems our broken, sin-laden bodies sometimes have trouble complying. Even if we were successful and popped out a few kids, eventually our fertility ends, often taking with it a piece of who we thought we were. The question becomes, can we rely on God to get us through even this?

Faith comes in two forms: faith toward future things (what we hope for) and faith toward invisible things (what we do not see). When we are certain God is in control of each area, and we live as if He is in control, that's faith. The way we envision God will determine the shape of our faith. If we see a big, faithful, all-powerful God, then our faith will rise to those levels. If, on the other hand, we see a smaller God, a distant or less active God, then our faith will plateau accordingly. My choice is to see a *big* God who is faithful, powerful, loving, and in control of all my circumstances. What about you?

The *Top Five Secrets* for Handling Reproductive Challenges

1. Be informed about options and treatments—don't just take your doctor's word for it.
2. Try to avoid resentment at friends who don't understand.
3. Seek help in the form of counseling or a support group if your loneliness or depression becomes unbearable.
4. Avoid taking out your negative emotions on your family.
5. Pray—even when you are mad at God or even doubting His existence.

Meditate on These Scriptures

For great is your love, reaching to the heavens; your faithfulness reaches to the skies.

Psalm 57:10

For you created my inmost being;
>   you knit me together in my mother's womb.
I praise you because I am fearfully and wonderfully made;
>   your works are wonderful,
>   I know that full well.

Psalm 139:13-14

A Prayer for Today

Dear Lord,

I praise You for the intricate nature of our bodies, which You created with a perfect design for us to go forth and multiply. I thank you for the awesome gift of motherhood. I know that as I experience the end of my fertility, whether soon or in the distant future, I may feel some sense of loss. I ask You to be with me, help me to deal with those feelings as well as physical symptoms, and help me to move into the next stage of my life with grace and gratitude. Above all, no matter what happens, let me always remember that You are faithful, and You are good.

Amen.

10

The Sandwich Showdown

SECRETS FOR CARING FOR AGING PARENTS

Emma, age forty-five, mother of two, has her plate full. Her family and parents seemed to always need her at the same time.

> *Squished; that's how I felt— between a rock and a hard place. My plate seemed so full it was overflowing. My family, my ill parents, my work, our home— it's all closing in on me. This, of course, was not my first encounter with overload. Today was one of those days it just seemed unbearable.* How will I navigate this circumstance? *I wondered.*
>
> *I had to take a mid-life mom time-out. For just thirty minutes I sat with my journal and pen in hand, my Bible on one side and my calendar on the other. Exhale. Breathe slowly. Pray. Regroup. It helps. My situation didn't change; my attitude did.*
>
> *That's my secret for managing what I refer to as my personal submarine sandwich. Why submarine? I often feel submerged in responsibility to my family.*

I was sitting in the ICU, my mother stretched out on the bed with wires and tubes everywhere. The last time I was in a hospital was when Sarah was born. Now my superhuman parents needed me urgently, and I was wondering if I was up to the challenge of being both a mid-life mom and a caretaker of elderly parents.

The situation had developed quickly, although in hindsight not unexpectedly. After Sarah was born, we were able to coax my mother and father to move to Texas to be near our family. It was wonderful for all of us. Sarah could know her maternal grandparents as well as Mark's parents, who lived nearby. My folks could enjoy their grand-daughter on a regular basis. And I could benefit from their company and wisdom—and the extra babysitting.

Then Mom had a heart attack. She was walking my brother's little girl in the stroller when she experienced sharp back pains and flu-like symptoms. The next day she found out that these flu-like feelings were actually a heart attack and that the damage was significant. Thus began our experience with stents, angioplasties, ICUs, and trying to accept the fact that Grand Mom was really sick. Heart disease. It doesn't go away; it's just managed.

Fortunately, Mom recovered. But her health reverted to the same critical situation several times within the next two years. Now her energy and her liveliness are tempered by multiple medications, side effects, and pain.

As my mother became sick, Mark's grandmother also began to decline. I had not known my grandparents, who had all died before I was born or when I was very young. In her nineties, Mark's grand-mother was my only picture of what a grandmother was like. Not being around aging individuals much, I had not seen how others dealt with their needs.

My mother-in-law's example of caregiving for an elderly family member was remarkable. As it became apparent that the time had come for her mother to stop living alone, she systematically began the process of cleaning out her mother's home, while my father-in-law prepared a lovely apartment for her in their home. It was a wake-up call for me—one day, would I be doing the same for my parents?

In my mind I still see my parents in their mid-forties, sort of frozen in time: wisdom-sharers and safety nets for those uncertain situations in life. They always appeared as superhuman, able to leap tall buildings with a single bound while balancing work, life, and two children. Now I'm forced to realize that *I'm* middle-aged and my parents are just human.

Being a member of the so-called "sandwich generation" is like living in a world of opposites. We watch our children grow stronger and increasingly independent while watching our moms and dads becoming weaker and more dependent. It can be a surreal feeling.

WHAT IS THE SANDWICH GENERATION?

Here's the bread: One slice is your parents; the other slice is your immediate family. The meat in the middle represents you and your issues. The lettuce, tomato, sprouts, and special sauce make up the extracurricular involvement that you call life.

National columnist Carol Abaya writes, "More than 25% of American families are involved in some way with elder/parent care. So if you are, know you are not alone."[1] She continues: "It's not easy to become elderly, or a parent to your parents. After all, our society says adults should be able to take care of themselves. But, as more live well into their eighties and nineties, and families are dispersed across the country, everyone is going to be involved somehow, some way, in elder care."

Given the demographics of our generation, building the sandwich isn't necessary—it has built itself. It's up to us to manage the serving, and sometimes we feel like we've bitten off more than we can chew. Mid-life moms struggling with responsibilities to parents, husbands, and children often feel a nagging sense that nothing is being done right. We can feel as if our hearts are being torn in two—our children on one side, our parents on the other, in a seemingly endless tug-of-war. The emotions involved are enormous: gratitude to those who were always there to help us; frustration at the loss of what was; resentment and anger at the lack of control; compassion for the sorrows and pains of others; and sometimes overwhelming personal stress.

J. Michael Dolan describes it as "a strenuous skirmish between your biological family and your fledgling family, both vying for your time, your emotions, and your money. It's a painful scenario that strains your relationships, alters your future and activates an annoying inner dialogue, which endlessly challenges your priorities."[2]

The transition into a season of caring for our parents doesn't always happen smoothly. We are deeply involved in the lives of our children—whether it's diapers and bottles or soccer and sleep-away camp—and suddenly we have to switch gears. We may be needed to help with our parents' routine needs such as shopping, transportation, and meals. We might be helping with medical care, or sitting by their bedsides. We are often needed to help with finances, both by contributing money and by helping with organization and bill paying. Whatever the level of involvement, it usually adds up to an immense and often unexpected complication of an already hectic life. But how do we know exactly *what* our responsibilities are?

HONOR THY FATHER AND MOTHER

As Christians, we're well aware of the fifth commandment as expressed in Deuteronomy 5:16: "Honor your father and your mother, as the LORD your God has commanded you, so that you may live long and that it may go well with you in the land the LORD your God is giving you." As a grown child of aging parents, what does it mean to honor them?

Obviously, one way to honor them is to help provide for their physical, financial, or material needs when they're older and less able to take care of themselves. Another way to honor them is to show them respect and allow them their dignity, regardless of their health or even declining mental and emotional capacity. Notice the Scripture points out that we are to honor *as God has commanded us*. It's not an option and it's not qualified, as in "Honor your parents if you feel like it" or "if you have a good relationship with them."

In fact, did you notice the commandment doesn't tell us to *love* our parents? God is well aware of the complicated parent-child relationship. He knows that by the time we're in mid-life, our relationship with our own parents might be anywhere on the spectrum from "best friends" to "strained" to "openly hostile." But He still insists we honor them. We cannot ignore them in their time of need; neither can we rationalize that our lives are too busy or our parents don't deserve our help. God is very clear about our responsibility to our parents, and He emphasizes this by indicating there will be a reward for following this commandment—"that you may live long and that it may go well with you." I love this because it shows that He understands this might be a tough one! Do you realize that this is the only one of the Ten Commandments in which He specifically promises a reward? It's as if God is saying, "I know this might be hard—even harder than avoiding adultery or murder—so I'm going to give you extra incentive." I think God had us mid-life moms in mind when He wrote this one on the tablet!

So, knowing it's our divinely mandated responsibility to honor our parents, how can we cope with the challenges? First, I think it's important to acknowledge that honoring our parents doesn't mean we have to do everything ourselves. We women tend to fall into the "dutiful daughter" role (otherwise known as "martyr"), and we think nothing will get done properly unless *we're* the ones doing it. But it's crucial to be realistic about what we can handle and how heavy a load our families can bear. We're obligated to see that our parents are appropriately cared for—not to do every bit of the labor ourselves. Later in this chapter I'm going to talk about ways to get help caring for aging parents, but right now I think it's important to get this fact through our heads: We don't do anybody any good if we overload ourselves or our families—emotionally, physically, or financially.

Another thing that can help us cope with the unique challenges of "sandwiching" is to realize that honoring our parents doesn't just mean taking care of them—it means honoring the values and morals they taught us. By taking good care of our husbands and children, and by living upright, ethical, and moral lives, we honor the way our parents raised us. Still, conflicts can arise when the expectations and needs of both our parents and our children intensify at the same time. We need some way to prioritize and make sure we're covering all the bases.

KEEPING OUR PRIORITIES STRAIGHT

In 1 Timothy 3, Paul recommends that a person being considered for leadership in the church "must manage his own family well and see that his children obey him with proper respect. (If anyone does not know how to manage his own family, how can he take care of God's church?)" (verses 4-5). Now I know that Paul is giving instructions for choosing church deacons. But I've always thought this was good advice from the apostle on gauging a person's spiritual maturity and leadership capability. So I ask myself, Am I managing my own family well? Not only is this a way to honor my parents, it's also a prerequisite for being able to offer them support and assistance. If my own household is in shambles, I won't be of much help to anyone else.

In talking to other mid-life moms who've found themselves smack in the middle of the "sandwich," I've learned that one of the most important secrets to success is to prioritize the homefront. So in the midst of honoring our aging parents, we need to:

1. *Protect our marriage.* It is so easy to abandon the niceties— the romance—in marriage when we're preoccupied. But we know that if our marriage is neglected, pretty soon everything else seems

to fall apart, too. As difficult or impossible as it may seem, making the effort to go out on dates with Hubby and spend special alone time with him helps us stay strong and refreshed for all our other duties.

2. *Protect our children.* The pull between the needs of our parents and the needs of our children can be devastating. But if forced to choose, I think we can *honor* our parents and their effort to raise us right by making the choice to give our children first place. There are many people who can assist us in caring for our parents, such as adult siblings and community resources, but nobody can give our children the special love and attention that we can. I'm certainly not suggesting we use our children as an excuse to abandon our parents! We simply need to protect our children from being neglected due to our overwhelming responsibilities. It's important that our children don't develop resentment toward their grandparents, which could happen if our children perceive that the grandparents are getting more of our attention. It's a fine line, but in the never-ending struggle for balance, I think our children weigh in a little more heavily.

3. *Protect our emotional, physical, and spiritual selves.* We've talked a lot in this book about taking time out for ourselves. Spending time alone with our Lord, taking care of our health, and nurturing ourselves emotionally are just as important when we're in the "sandwich." In fact, it's not uncommon for mid-life moms in the midst of caring for the generations both above and below them to end up in the hospital themselves! So this is not a platitude—I'm not paying lip service to the old "take time out to nurture yourself" line. It's serious business! I've said it before, but if we don't take care of ourselves, nobody will— and we run a greater risk of letting everyone else down.

4. *Protect our jobs.* A large number of mid-life moms are truly "doing it all." They're working outside the home, raising school-age children, and caring for aging parents. An often-overlooked casualty of this situation is the job, which we most likely can't afford to lose, especially if we're contributing financially to both our own household and our parents'. In fact, over half of elder-caregivers have some type of workplace problem as a result of their caregiving role.[3] To avoid this, we need to keep the lines of communication open with our employers as much as possible, seeking flexibility and understanding. We can also avail ourselves of help from relatives and friends, so that we don't endanger our livelihood.

We've gotten deep into the discussion about priorities in previous chapters, but knowing and living our priorities becomes even more crucial when our caregiving obligations multiply. Now more than ever, our reliance on the Lord to keep us strong is what will make the difference in our effectiveness. Thus we need spiritual checks and balances to keep us sharp. When we miss several days of quiet time with the Lord, we know it. When we miss several weeks of seeking God, everybody else knows it. This is a good time not only to seek Him, but to lean on Him. We can also lean on others whom He provides to help us.

ASKING FOR HELP

I've alluded several times to the reality that we can't do all this caregiving ourselves. But when you're in the middle of a sandwich situation, it's hard to know where to turn, and it might just seem easier to do it, rather than figure out a way to delegate it. Mid-life mom Darla relates, "I had teenage twins who were going through major adolescent issues at the same time that my mother was sick and needed me by her side. It was truly the most awful year of my life. I was yanked back and forth so much, and no matter what I did, everyone was dissatisfied. My daughter and my mother both wanted *more* of me—but there was only so much of me to go around."

Darla felt like she was in a no-win situation. There was no way to delegate because everyone wanted *her* and no one else would do. In this situation, the best way to get help is to try and farm out as many "nonrelationship" responsibilities as possible. Can you afford to have someone take over the housecleaning responsibilities for a while? Can someone at your church organize a casserole-brigade to help your family out with dinners periodically? Can your husband pitch in more than usual, whether it's in the area of childcare, laundry, or cooking? We need to think creatively rather than always falling into the "only I can do it" trap.

Another area in which we might need to ask for help is coping with the unique stresses of inter-generational caregiving. If your sandwich situation is causing a great deal of anxiety and conflict in your family, enlisting the help of a family therapist could make the difference between barely surviving and thriving. It may be difficult to make the time, but an hour with a counselor each week or every two weeks for a couple months can really help family members communicate their needs and get better at finding solutions to tough dilemmas. One study revealed that in families that sought professional support through counseling, particularly for the caregiving mother, the children showed less depression and increased social competence.[4]

Finally, the biggest area in which we might need to ask for help is in the actual care of the older generation. The first thing we need to consider seriously is whether there are other adults in the family, or in our parents' church community, who can help with whatever needs to be done. Family members who don't live close to the aging parents might be able to contribute financially. Neighbors and friends who live close to them could be asked to help with things such as transportation to doctor's appointments, meals, and simply checking in to make sure they're okay. While it sometimes feels like more trouble than it's worth to try and round up a whole "gang" of helpers, most people enjoy being given a specific task that can be helpful, and it really can take a load off your shoulders. If nothing else, just remember—it never hurts to ask!

Here are a few other ways you can solicit help with caring for the older generation:

5. *Hire in-home help.* I know several people who have used Meals on Wheels and find it to be very helpful. Many people hire in-home care, whether an hour a day or round-the-clock care is necessary. Home care comes in all forms. You can hire a registered nurse, an occupational therapist, a home health aide who assists in activities of daily living such as dressing and bathing, or even a home chore worker. It's important to screen possible helpers carefully. Use a website such as www.careguide.com to help find the appropriate help.

6. *Utilize community programs and services.* Contact city or state agencies and check your yellow pages under Assisted Living and Elder Care Services. Many cities have free buses that provide transportation for seniors, as well as other programs that provide meals, in-home help, and recreation.

7. *Help your parent get involved in a local senior center.* These are places where the elderly can get together to talk, play games such as bingo, go on fun outings, and be with others, as opposed to being isolated at home. One of the most important determinants of health in the elderly is the number of social contacts the person has. It might take some nudging to get them socially involved, but doing so can greatly increase their chances for thriving.

8. *Determine whether you need to consider a nursing home.* This may be a very difficult decision, involving guilt and feelings of inadequacy on your part, along with fear and resistance on your parent's part. If you do need to choose some kind of retirement, nursing, or assisted-living home, you'll feel best about your choice if you screen your options carefully. Interview staff members, ensure the establishment offers plenty of activities to keep residents engaged, and look for a low ratio of residents to staff members.

9. *Consider hiring a financial consultant.* One of the most awkward parts of caring for our parents can be our involvement in their finances. This is a good time to seek professional help in organizing both their finances and your own, especially if the households are going to be merged in any way.

10. *Hire a Geriatric Care Manager.* These are people who specialize in coordinating services and handling the logistics that

can be a nightmare for a sandwiched mom with multiple obligations. Hospital social workers and home health nurses can give you a referral, or your can check your yellow pages under Nursing or Social Services.

Most of us are naturally inclined to take the weight of our entire family—all generations—on our own shoulders. Keep in mind that everyone in the family benefits when we realistically assess our capabilities and delegate (or hire out) as many obligations as possible. Whether we're doing all the caregiving ourselves or soliciting help, our relationship with the elder generation hangs in the balance. How do we cope with this new era in our bond with our parents?

Parenting Our Parents

Over the years, our relationship with our parents (or in-laws) has evolved into whatever it is today. You may view your parents with respect, admiration, and love, or you may be having a much more difficult time, dealing with resentment, bad memories, and general dysfunction. These issues can be worse than the primary caregiving responsibilities, and if we haven't dealt with them yet, there's no time like the present. We may need professional help or just some serious sit-down time with God, but it's time to let go of the past so we can deal with our parents in the present.

One of the biggest keys to a successful adult relationship with our parents is *forgiveness*. We all have things we need to forgive in our parents. If you're walking around in a state of resentment, fear, and disappointment, it will be very difficult for you to honor your parents in their waning years. Now is the time to think about forgiveness, even if it means a year or two of psychotherapy.

Forgiveness doesn't mean acceptance of bad behavior. It means we wipe the slate clean and choose not to remember and harbor a grudge. Is this always easy? No! It may seem particularly impossible if you were a victim of abuse, addictions, abandonment, or adultery in childhood. But Jesus commands us to forgive, because He knows we need it for our own mental and emotional health.

As Acts 10:43 reminds us, "Everyone who believes in him receives forgiveness of sins through his name." As we receive unlimited forgiveness from the Father through Jesus Christ, we are also commanded to extend that forgiveness to others. True forgiveness creates a new foundation and a new beginning for the relationship. Every time you forgive, you please God and you create new mental health for yourself; you have chosen to continue a relationship without the excess drama of the past.

What are some other ways to nurture the relationship with our parents, even as we become involved in taking care of them? Here are a few tips I've gathered:

11. *Don't think you're parenting your parents.* One of the ways we honor our father and mother is to give them respect and allow them the dignity of always being our parents. We may be assisting them; we may be heavily involved in caretaking; but they're still our parents. We need to be mindful of our attitude in approaching them, not belittling them or making them feel like children.

12. *Deal with conflicts before they get out of hand.* As in all relationships, communication is key. We need to be honest and upfront,

while at the same time caring and sensitive. If problems are occurring, we need to discuss them A.S.A.P. to avoid them getting out of hand. One of the most frequent problems I hear about is when the sandwiched-mom is doing everything humanly possible, yet her own parent accuses her of not doing enough. In this situation, it's sometimes necessary to put our foot down and gently let everyone know that we have limits.

13. *Make sure your parents understand that you're on their side.* Health and aging problems can be frightening, and when they see you jumping through hoops to arrange doctor appointments, home health care, and assisted living arrangements, they may feel you're trying to abandon them. Talk candidly with them about their needs and how you're trying to help. Help them understand you're *not* trying to get rid of the responsibility of taking care of them; you're simply trying to get them the best care possible based on your own limited time and money resources.

14. *Involve your parents in all aspects of their own care.* If they're mentally competent, ask for their input as much as possible. Discuss all arrangements with them and encourage them to make decisions. This can be challenging because often elderly parents insist they want *you* and no one else to take care of them. If this is the case, gently but firmly explain that it's not possible, and continue to encourage their own decision-making. As adults, they still should be taking some responsibility for themselves, to whatever level they're capable of.

15. *Remember that this situation is difficult for your parents, too.* Let's face it, getting old is a rotten deal. You can lose your independence, your health, your mental capacity, not to mention your spouse

and many of your friends. It's a scary place to be, and we can hardly blame our parents for wanting us, their children, with them at this difficult time. We have to give them leeway if they're frustrated, angry, or depressed. We just need to do our best to give them as much support and understanding as possible.

THE GOOD NEWS

The bottom line is, being in the "sandwich showdown" could just be the most difficult time of your life. It also offers opportunities for unparalleled growth and taking your relationship with your parents to new levels. If you must suffer through a parent's major illness and death, it can be devastatingly sad and yet gloriously fulfilling to be there for a parent in their last days.

While our culture has the reputation for disregarding our elderly, my experience is that most adult children are not abandoning their aging parents. It is heartwarming to see the lengths to which women are going to satisfy the demands of their own children and their parents at the same time. Miraculously, research even shows that families in the midst of intergenerational caregiving experience increasing marital happiness.[5] So even though we're stretched at both ends, many of us seem to be holding it together pretty well. I always like hearing good news!

Just one more thought on being in the sandwich generation. Isn't this a good time to look ahead at our own future and think about the ways our own aging might be handled? Will we expect our own children to take care of us, or will we somehow manage to retain our independence? Are we providing *right now* for our future financial situation? Will we have enough in our retirement accounts to cover whatever medical care or assisted living we might need? How can we prepare emotionally for the day when our own children are not realistically able to care for us, and we must depend on strangers?

I've come to the conclusion that one of the best gifts we can give our children is to prepare ahead of time for our own old age. And hopefully, when our offspring are themselves in the midst of mid-life motherhood (or fatherhood), they will be spared some of the anguish of helping their parents—us—grow old.

The *Top Five Secrets* for Caring for Aging Parents

1. Don't be afraid to ask for help, including hiring professional caregivers.
2. Realize you're not going to be perfect all the time.
3. Clean up your relationship with your parents the best you can, in light of your own situation.
4. Be sure to continue giving your husband and children top priority.
5. Ask for God's help and strength on a daily basis.

Meditate on These Scriptures

Two are better than one, because they have a good return for their work: If one falls down, his friend can help him up. But pity the man who falls and has no one to help him up! Also, if two lie down together, they will keep warm. But how can one keep warm alone? Though one may be overpowered, two can defend themselves. A cord of three strands is not quickly broken.

Ecclesiastes 4:9-12

An angel from heaven appeared to him and strengthened him.

Luke 22:43

A Prayer for Today

Dear Lord,

I acknowledge I cannot handle everything in my own strength. I admit my own insufficiency, and I rest in the knowledge that You do not give us burdens we are unable to bear. Please strengthen me, and give me the courage to take on all the tasks You have set before me. Give me wisdom to know how to juggle my roles in the best way possible. Give me compassion to care for those who are suffering. Let me reflect Your endless love to others in all that I do.

Amen.

Conqueror Queens

Hey sisters, we're more than conquerors, right? Doesn't God say so in His Word (see Romans 8:37)? So why should we let the trials of mid-life get us down? Through Him who loves us, we are bigger than any challenge that comes before us. Shouldn't we be looking at mid-life motherhood through God's eyes?

God views our lives as a tapestry. He has created the design, and He is in control. Unfortunately, we see only glimpses of the Master's work, and we often view it from the backside. We see the unclipped strings, the knots, the frays, the ugly parts. Seeing the challenges as part of the Master's plan is the secret of successful living.

As I struggled to write this book in a positive tone, I kept hitting the proverbial wall. Not just writer's block, but full-strength "life block." I often felt less than positive about this mid-life juncture in my life's journey. I didn't want to hear trite sayings, and I had trouble putting a positive spin on what I viewed as a very difficult time of life.

You see, while writing this book, I became pregnant again. Now that I'm in my forties, I knew this would be my last hurrah, our last chance to give our daughter a sibling, to experience the joy of holding a baby again. But the pregnancy was short-lived and resulted in a miscarriage. Depression and sadness over the loss totally engulfed my spirit. Time has passed and I have a clearer view—still a vacant uterus, but a clearer view. Perhaps this has happened to you—maybe not the exact same circumstance, perhaps something more tragic.

But through the process of researching mid-life, talking to countless mid-life moms, and writing this book, I've discovered that mid-life truly can be viewed as an exciting new beginning. It's the start of the second half of our life here on earth. Shouldn't we as believers take the bull by the horns and finish strong? Regrettably, many of us allow ourselves to be beaten down by circumstances instead of claiming our inheritance as conquerors.

A friend may ask, "How are you doing?" We answer, "Well, under the circumstances, okay, I guess." Maybe a fake smile to go along with it. That was me, many times over the last couple of years since my fortieth birthday. I've finally discovered that I really can choose to move out from under that load. I never would have believed it, but through prayer and the support of many mid-life friends, I'm finding my way back to abundant living. It didn't happen without tears, painful days, and sincere cries to God for direction. But I'm certain that if it can happen to me, it can happen to you.

An unexpected advantage of writing this book was the encouragement I received from my editor at NavPress as she shared her thoughts about her mid-life mothering experience. Upbeat and enthusiastic about life in general, she helped me to get out of the doldrums and just get up and dance. As together we shaped this book, I was able to take a deep breath and move toward thinking positively about my life and my future. Thanks, Rachelle.

Author and motivational speaker Zig Ziglar says, "Where you start is not as important as where you finish."[1] We've come a long way from where we started, but will we flourish in the finish? I think of this time in my life as the "beginning of the finish." How wonderful if we could say at the end of our lives, like the apostle Paul, "I have fought the good fight, I have finished the race, I have kept the faith" (2 Timothy 4:7).

As I look back over our "secrets" for successful mid-life motherhood, I can't help thinking that this unique time of our lives offers incredible opportunities for growth and for joy. In the midst of the ups and downs, the highs and the lows, I keep these little reminders running through my brain:

- Our friends keep us sane. We need to nurture those relationships.
- Spending time alone with God is crucial to all other aspects of our lives.
- Our families are our top priorities after our relationship with Jesus.
- We have developed wisdom over the years, and we have the responsibility to use it.
- Having more patience than when we were younger helps life run much more smoothly.
- Our age and awareness of the passing of time makes us able to treasure every moment more fully as a gift from God.
- Knowing how to nurture ourselves takes the pressure off our family members and makes us much more pleasant people.
- Refusing to worry about aging is not only helpful, it's what Jesus desires.
- When we "think young" we feel better and can actually slow our own mental and emotional aging process.

• We can acknowledge the hard parts of life without wasting time
  dwelling on them.

I have finally come to the conclusion that mid-life motherhood is
all about attitude. I have the choice to develop an *attitude* with *alti-
tude*. "But those who hope in the LORD will renew their strength.
They will soar on wings like eagles; they will run and not grow weary,
they will walk and not be faint" (Isaiah 40:31). Sounds good, huh?
Let's put our hope in the Lord and prepare to soar, okay? Up, up, and
away. See you in the clouds.

Meditate on These Scriptures

I pray also that the eyes of your heart may be enlightened in
order that you may know the hope to which he has called you, the
riches of his glorious inheritance in the saints, and his incompa-
rably great power for us who believe.

Ephesians 1:18

So we fix our eyes not on what is seen, but on what is unseen. For
what is seen is temporary, but what is unseen is eternal.

2 Corinthians 4:18

A Prayer for Today

Dear Lord,

Thank you for the gift of life both on this earth and for eternity. Please guide and direct our choices. Help us to consistently
seek Your wisdom, and Your power for Your glory.

Amen.

Mid-Life Mom Resources

Mom's Secret Weapons

Mothers of Preschoolers (MOPS)

A Christian organization dedicated to nurturing every mother of a preschooler through individual groups meeting all over the world, regional and national conventions.
www.MOPS.org

Hearts at Home

A Christian organization offering professional weekend conferences and a monthly newsletter to provide encouragement for the mother at home.
www.heart-at-home.org

Family and Home

For parents who forgo paid employment or cut back to engage in the challenges and joys of nurturing their children of all ages.
www.familyandhome.org

At Home Mothers

Practical information, inspiration, services, support, and encouragement for the mother at home and those who want to be.
www.athomemothers.com

Between Friends

Tips, techniques, and articles designed to help you do more with less
and save time in the process.
www.Betweenfriends.org

PARENTING

Homebodies

One-stop resource for encouragement and insights for parents who
have decided to take time out to nourish their most important
resource—their kids—in the best workplace ever—their homes.
www.homebodies.org

Parent Soup

A vast resource for families from birthdays to biting. Parenting information, recipes, ages and stages, relationships.
www.parentsoup.com

Parent Place

Ideas, articles, recipes, and more. Another comprehensive resource for effective parenting.
www.parentplace.com

Focus on the Family

The Christian icon for family issues. Articles, family and relationship advice, and daily radio programs to help guide us as parents and believers.
www.focusonthefamily.org

Family Fun

An on-line magazine featuring craft ideas, recipes, vacation recommendations all for the family.
www.familyfun.com

SINGLE MID-LIFE MOMS

SingleRose.com

Multiple resources for single mothers.
www.singlerose.com

Divorce Care

A support-group guide. Where you can find help as you recover from the hurt of divorce.
www.divorcecare.com

Single Christian Moms

Articles, ideas, and support for single mothers.
www.suite101.com

MID-LIFE MOM IN THE MARKETPLACE

Working Mother

An online magazine offering tips on balance of work and home.
Features foods, self-improvement, and children's articles.
www.workingmother.com

Blue Suit Mom

Offers information and tools to help executive mothers find balance
with work and family.
www.bluesuitmom.com

Mothers and More

For sequencing mothers—balancing work and home.
www.mothersandmore.com

The Entrepreneurial Parent

Resources for combining family and work.
www.en-parent.com

The National Association of Child Care Resources
and Referral Agencies

A site for assisting families as they look for safe and excellent care for
their children.

www.naccrra.org

Child Care Aware

A site to help parents stay on top of their child care issues.

www.childcareaware.org

BABIES AT MID-LIFE

Having Children over Forty

Advice, prenatal care, and what to expect for the mother over forty.

www.over40babies@yahoo.com

BabyZone.com

Large on-line neighborhood of resources for women from pre-
pregnancy through delivery and their kids zero to three years old.

www.babyzone.com

Mid-Life Mother

Offers discussion on mid-life pregnancy and parenting.

www.mid-lifemother.com

Postpartum Support International

A site designed to help women after the birth of their child.
www.postpartum.net

CARING FOR AGING PARENTS AT MID-LIFE

Family Care Alliance

Advice, articles, and more for elder adult care.
www.caregiver.org

The National Association for Area Agencies on Aging/Eldercare Locator

A locator service for elder care.
www.aahsa.org

Notes

Introduction

1. Dr. David Demko, PhD, "Mean Age Moms, Ladies In Waiting," *AgeVenture News Service* (December 12, 2002), p. 1.
2. Rita Rubin, "A Wrinkle on Motherhood," *USA Today*, 23 January, 2003, sec. D, p. 1.
3. Rubin, p. 1.
4. According to the National Center for Health Statistics.
5. Alexandra Rockey Fleming, "Welcoming the Stork Later in Life," *Insight on the News* (December 11, 2000), p. 10.
6. Ephesians 1:18.

Chapter One

1. *Merriam Webster's Collegiate Dictionary,* 10th ed., s.v. "patience."
2. Song, "Soak Up the Sun" by Sheryl Crow.

Chapter Two

1. *Merriam Webster's Collegiate Dictionary,* 10th ed., s.v. "crisis."
2. Barbara Sher, *It's Only Too Late If You Don't Start Now* (New York: Dell (Random House), 1998), p. xiii.
3. Brenda Poinsett, *What Will I Do with the Rest of My Life?* (Colorado Springs: NavPress, 2000), p. 12.

4. Christiane Northrup, *The Wisdom of Menopause* (New York: Doubleday, 2003), p. 78.

5. Sher, p. xiv.

6. Northrup, p. 78.

7. Northrup, p. 76.

8. Rick Warren, *The Purpose Driven Life* (Grand Rapids, Mich.: Zondervan, 2002), p. 45.

CHAPTER THREE

1. Rob and Diane Parsons, *The Sixty Minute Mother* (Nashville, Tenn.: Broadman & Holman, 2002), p. 60.

2. Charles E. Hummel, *Freedom from Tyranny of the Urgent* (Downers Grove, Ill.: InterVarsity, 1997), p. 46.

3. Penelope J. Stokes, *Simple Words of Wisdom: 52 Virtues for Every Woman* (Nashville, Tenn.: J Countryman, 1998), p. 23.

4. Nancy London, *Hot Flashes and Warm Bottles* (Berkley, Calif.: Celestial Arts, 2001), p. 57.

5. Arlene Rossen Cardozo, *Sequencing* (New York: Collier, 1986).

6. Personal note from Bob Rognlien to Rachelle Gardner, May 19, 2003.

CHAPTER FOUR

1. Ruth Klein, M.S., *Manage Your Time/Market Your Business* (New York: AMACOM, 1995), p. 23.

2. Jeffrey P. Davidson, et al., *The Complete Idiot's Guide to Managing Your Time* (Indianapolis, Ind.: Alpha Books, 1995), p. 32.

3. Davidson, p. 10.

4. Julie Morgenstern, *Time Management from the Inside Out: the Foolproof System for Taking Control of Your Schedule and Your Life* (New York: Henry Holt, 2000), p. 57. (Julie Morgenstern is owner of New York City organizing firm Task Masters.)

CHAPTER FIVE

1. Anne Morrow Lindbergh, *Gift From the Sea* (New York: Pantheon Books, 1975), p. 25.

CHAPTER SIX

1. Edgar Guest, "I'd Rather See a Sermon" in *The Speakers Treasury of Four Hundred Quotable Poems,* Croft M.Pentz, ed. (Grand Rapids Mich.: Zondervan, 1963, public domain), p. 159.

2. Elisa Morgan and Carol Kuykendall, *What Every Child Needs* (Grand Rapids, Mich.: Zondervan, 1997), p. 45.

3. Karol Ladd, *The Power of a Positive Women* (Monroe, La.: Howard, 2002), p. 63.

4. Elizabeth George, *A Woman After God's Own Heart* (Eugene, Ore.: Harvest House, 1998).

CHAPTER SEVEN

1. Dr. Phil McGraw, *Life Strategies: Doing What Works, Doing What Matters* (New York: Hyperion, 2000), p. 102.

2. From *Building Health and Youthfulness* by Paul Bragg (Health Science, 1978, Out of Print).

3. Brad Schoenfeld, *Look Great Sleeveless* (New York: Prentice Hall, 2002), p. 42.

4. Christiane Northrup, *The Wisdom of Menopause* (New York: Doubleday, 2003), p. 65.

5. "The Effects of Stress on Your Body," WebMd Health, http://my.webmd.com/content/pages/7/1674_52147.htm?lasts-electedguid={5FE84E90-BC77-4056-A91C-9531713CA348}. Accessed on August 6, 2003.

CHAPTER EIGHT

1. Vicki Iovine, *The Girlfriends' Guide to Getting Your Groove Back: Loving Your Family Without Losing Your Mind* (New York: Perigree, 2001), p. 94.

2. From www.brainyquote.com.

3. Gary Chapman, *The Five Love Languages* (Chicago: Northfield Publishers, 1992, 1995), p. 97.

4. Bill and Lynne Hybels, *Fit to Be Tied* (Grand Rapids, Mich.: Zondervan, 1992), p. 100.

5. H. Norman Wright, *The Secrets of a Lasting Marriage* (Ventura, Calif.: Regal, 1995), p. 153.

6. Karen Scalf Linamen, *Pillow Talk: The Intimate Marriage from A to Z* (Grand Rapids, Mich.: Baker, 1998), p. 61.

7. David and Claudia Arp, *The Second Half of Marriage* (Grand Rapids, Mich.: Zondervan, 1996), p. 27.

Chapter Nine

1. Doreen Nagle, *But I Don't* Feel *Too Old to Be a Mommy*
   (Deerfield Beach, Fla.: Health Communications, Inc., 2002), p.
   xxiii.
2. Nagle, p. 214.

Chapter Ten

1. Quoted in Doreen Nagle, *But I Don't* Feel *Too Old to Be a*
   Mommy (Deerfield Beach, Fla.: Health Communications, Inc.,
   2002), p. xxiii.
2. J. Michael Dolan, *How to Care for Your Aging Parents and Still*
   Have a Life of Your Own (Los Angeles, Calif.: Mulholland
   Pacific, 1992), p. 10.
3. Gwen Moran, quoted in "Being Squeezed in the Sandwich
   Generation." Report from the National Alliance for Caregiving
   and Metropolitan Life Insurance. Website bluesuitmom.com.
   (http://www.bluesuitmom.com/family/relationships/
   caregiving.html) Accessed on September 10, 2003.
4. Christine A. Price, "Aging Families Series Bulletin #2: The
   Sandwich Generation," Ohio State Univerisity. Website
   http://www.hec.ohio-state.edu/famlife/aging/PDFs/ Sandwich%
   20Generation.final.pdf. Accessed on September 9, 2003.
5. Christine A. Price, "Aging Families Series Bulletin #2: The
   Sandwich Generation," Ohio State Univerisity. Website
   http://www.hec.ohio-state.edu/famlife/aging/PDFs/ Sandwich%
   20Generation.final.pdf. Accessed on September 9, 2003.

EPILOGUE

1. "Best Inspirational Quotes," online. http://www.bestinspirationalquotes.com/success-leaders/zig-ziglar.htm. Accessed on September 9, 2003.

About the Author

JANE JARRELL, a forty-plus mother of an elementary school-age daughter, is a popular Christian radio, TV, and conference speaker. She is a charter member of the MOPS National Speakers Bureau. She has authored eleven books, including *Mom Matters*. Jane and her family make their home in Richardson, Texas.

Her readers may e-mail her at jane.jarrell@prodigy.net.

A MOTHER'S READING IS NEVER DONE.

A Mother's Heart

Being a mother is an important job, but one that can easily feel frustrating and under appreciated. Learn how to become the godly mother God designed you to be.
by Jean Fleming

Train Up a Mom

Filled with real-life stories, encouragement, and tips, this Bible study will teach you the importance of living a godly life in order to raise godly children.
by Vollie Sanders

A Mother's Legacy

Women of the Bible struggled with motherhood in much the same way mothers do today. Learn from ten biblical women whose struggles and victories are as real today as they were centuries ago.
by Jeanne Hendricks

To get your copies, visit your local bookstore, call 1-800-366-7788, or log on to www.navpress.com. Ask for a FREE catalog of NavPress products. Offer BPA.

NAVPRESS ®
BRINGING TRUTH TO LIFE
www.navpress.com